AN HUMBLER HEAVEN

The Reigning Error:
The Crisis of World Inflation

An Humbler Heaven

THE BEGINNINGS OF HOPE

WILLIAM REES-MOGG

Lo! the poor Indian, whose untutor'd mind
Sees God in clouds, or hears him in the wind;
His soul proud Science never taught to stray
Far as the Solar walk, or Milky way,
Yet simple Nature to his hope has giv'n,
Behind the cloud-topt hill, an humbler Heav'n . . .
ALEXANDER POPE. *An Essay on Man. Epistle I. 1733.*

HAMISH HAMILTON

LONDON

First published in Great Britain 1977
by Hamish Hamilton Ltd
90 Great Russell Street London WC1B 3PT
Second Impression November 1977

SBN 241 89692 4

Printed and bound in Great Britain by
REDWOOD BURN LIMITED
Trowbridge & Esher

TO GILLIAN

THERE IS one glory of the sun, and another glory of the moon, and another glory of the stars; for one star differeth from another star in glory. So also is the resurrection of the dead. It is sown in corruption; it is raised in incorruption: it is sown in dishonour; it is raised in glory: it is sown in weakness; it is raised in power; it is sown a natural body; it is raised a spiritual body. There is a natural body, and there is a spiritual body. And so it is written, the first man Adam was made a living soul; the last Adam was made a quickening spirit. Howbeit that was not first which is spiritual, but that which is natural; and afterwards that which is spiritual. The first man is of the earth, earthy: the second man is the Lord from heaven. As is the earthy, such are they also that are earthy: and as is the heavenly, such are they also that are heavenly. And as we have borne the image of the earthy, we shall also bear the image of the heavenly. Now this I say, brethren, that flesh and blood cannot inherit the kingdom of God; neither doth corruption inherit incorruption. Behold I show you a mystery; we shall not all sleep, but we shall all be changed, in a moment, in the twinkling of an eye, at the last trump: for the trumpet shall sound, and the dead shall be raised incorruptible, and we shall be changed. For this corruptible must put on incorruption, and this mortal must put on immortality. So when this corruptible shall have put on incorruption, and this mortal shall have put on immortality, then shall be brought to pass the saying that is written, Death is swallowed up in victory. O death where is thy sting? O grave where is thy victory? The sting of death is sin: and the strength of sin is the law. But thanks be to God, which giveth us the victory through our Lord Jesus Christ. Therefore, my beloved brethren, be ye steadfast, immovable, always abounding in the work of the Lord, forasmuch as you know that your labour is not in vain in the Lord.

St. Paul I Corinthians 15 (verses 41 to 58)

I

THE BELIEF in God is something which grows like a mustard seed in the human mind. It starts as a hope; it is nourished by love; it matures into faith. In the great saints can be seen the full development of the psychological process, the process St. Paul describes as the change from the natural to the spiritual, from the first Adam to the last. Yet in all religious lives there is the same psychology of development, if very imperfect and inadequate.

The growth of belief influences all parts of the personality; it is not only a development of ideas but must express itself also in action. Faith comes by grace; it is something given, not something earned. It comes to different people in different ways, but mostly through the experience of their senses, through actual observation of God's works, including particularly his work in human life. Very few men come to believe in God because of abstract argument, because very few men have intellects capable of following such arguments; they are not moved by abstractions which they do not understand. Few men are moved to believe in God through direct converse with God himself; that is reserved for Moses or the great mystics. The rest of us, the vast majority of us, come to believe in God, if we do, in the same way that we come to hold our other beliefs, as the result of what we are told, or learn, or experience.

I have always felt a checking diffidence in writing about religion, and for good reason. I am not a theologian, I have made no adequate spiritual preparation for the task, I do not feel myself to have spiritual qualifications for it.

I am in addition a member of that unilluminated group, the comfortably off, middle aged, English professional class. It is natural that people should choose us as their worldly

1

advisers, for we make some of the best lawyers or bankers that can be found, but for spiritual advisers we lack the essential qualifications. We are unhumble, unmeek and unpoor. Had we not produced our one great Saint in Sir Thomas More, I might regard my background as a final disqualification. As it is, I offer it as a warning. Anything that I write must be from a point of view that is in many ways spiritually inadequate.

As against this obvious unfitness, I feel justified in writing because there is no other subject that in the present state of the world seems so much worth writing about. As the Editor of a daily newspaper I have to report the affairs of a world which has lost its faith, which is like a fish out of water or a drowning man, desperately thrashing around for lack of oxygen. Since the time of Christ there has been no period in which there has been the same feeling of impoverishment, a spiritual impoverishment in which the richest nations are the poorest in spiritual terms.

At the same time the evidences of God in the world are what they always were. Men only have to open their eyes and their hearts and the love of God comes flooding in upon them. If the evidences which have influenced me were to influence a single other person, then I should have done him the greatest possible favour. As I have found these evidences overwhelmingly convincing in my own life, it is natural I should want to express them to other people, some of whom may perhaps have minds constituted like mine.

I was born on July 14th, 1928, the third child and only son of a land-owning family in Somerset. My father was a member of the Church of England, but not active, and had a great respect for the Roman Catholic Church, my mother's religion, in which I was brought up. My mother is of Irish-American descent and it is to her and to that descent I owe my Catholicism.

So far as I can remember I was not a particularly religious child; I recall the boredom and mild discomfort of attendance at Church; I fidgeted; I found confession difficult; I did not attend Mass regularly at my non-Catholic schools, though I took great pleasure in the Anglican services at Charterhouse, and as Head of the School I read the lessons with eloquence and only too much relish; I contemplated joining the Church of England, more, I am afraid, for reasons of ambition than of religion; I again attended Mass irregularly at Oxford, though I never wholly gave up the practice of my religion, nor my belief in it. I was lapsatory but never fully lapsed.

For some time I suffered from what I now recognize to have been a phase of adolescent depression, with morbid ideas of death and suicide and an indulgence in melancholy literature, including Christopher Marlowe, Edgar Allan Poe and even the harmless graveyard melancholy of Gray's Elegy. In short, so far as religion was concerned, I had a normal adolescence, with doubts and temptations and crazy ideas which can still give me a sharp stab of regret and remorse. I was a clever boy, and probably not as nasty as my worst memories suggest.

It was only after I came down from Oxford that my religious interests began, very slowly at first, to awaken. This happened by fortunate circumstance. For some ten years I shared a flat and then a house in London with my sister Anne; she had for some time before that been living in Chelsea, and we went to the Church of the Holy Redeemer in Cheyne Row, where the Priest in charge was Canon Alfonso de Zulueta.

When I first went there it was, so far as I can recall, because I thought I should accompany my sister, and because I was still a church-goer inside the family circle, if an irregular one outside it. However Father de Zulueta's Mass, with his impressive dignity and his intellectual sermons, was much more interesting to me than the humbler Irish Masses, with their simple homilies, had been. I do not think there is anything wrong in that; it is natural that an intellectual young man should prefer intellectually interesting sermons.

From that point on I resumed being at least a fairly regular church-goer. My religious life improved, though at first only from the verge of abstention to a Sunday by Sunday regularity not supported by much thought or weekday attention. By the time I was thirty I still had the religion of a child, without benefit of the child's innocence and simplicity. I certainly did not give religion the attention I gave to the ordinary worldly matters with which I was dealing; I would have thought it shameful to know as little about economics or politics or literature as I knew about religion. I never opened a religious book, though I was influenced and impressed by the religious

3

ideas of Jung, and particularly by a television programme in which he was interviewed by John Freeman.

I do not mean to suggest that I was a great sinner, for I was not. If I had to label the first three decades of my life I would say I went from being a happy child, to being a troubled schoolboy, to being a decent chap in my twenties. I am glad that I was at least that, inadequate as it was.

Gradually in that period religion did begin to take a stronger hold on me. I do not recall exactly the point at which my evening prayers again became regular, or when I would go to Mass on Sunday in a strange town. Those are small enough duties, but others who have been on the not uncommon road back from indifference will recognize them as significant stages on the way. I do know that at the beginning of the 1950s I did not go out of my way to attend Mass; by the end of the 1950s I was concerned to avoid missing Mass, though no doubt less than absolutely regular.

I married Gillian in March 1962, to my great happiness; my father-in-law Thomas Morris was then Mayor of St. Pancras; we were married at the Church of the Holy Redeemer, and had our reception at the Town Hall.

Already at the time of our wedding my father, to whom I was and since his death remain devoted, was seriously ill. He was barely able to last out the ceremony and reception, and after further deterioration in the summer he died on December 12th, 1962, five days before the birth of our eldest daughter, Emma, on December 17th. I went to the funeral from the maternity hospital, and back to the maternity hospital from the funeral.

There were incidents of that time which tended to accelerate changes that were already taking place in my attitude to religion. By the time of my marriage my attitude to religion had already changed, and both the happiness and the responsibilities of a loving marriage certainly developed it further. My wife is not a Catholic, but she has been better than most Catholics in supporting both my religious life and that of our, by now, four children.

I was much affected at the time by apparently psychic incidents associated with my father's death. All my life—or at least since the age of eleven—I have had premonitory dreams. The great majority of them have been like flashes of

4

trivial foreknowledge, absolutely convincing to anyone who has experienced them, absolutely unconvincing to anyone who has not. A few have been more important in their subject matter. I had a clear premonitory dream before my father's death, so clear and so convincing that I knew he was going to die for some ten months before he did so, and before it was at all clear that his illness, which was quite gradual, had entered its closing stage.

Not immediately after his death, but about fifteen months later, we lived briefly in the house in which he spent his last years, and our bedroom was the room in which he had died. I had then, not invariably in that room, brief periods of tranquillity and ecstasy, such as many people have experienced, such as convinced me of the harmony of the universe and the love of God. I have had such experiences elsewhere and at other times, but never so frequently and intensely as in that house then.

I do not attach too much importance to these experiences, though I believe they are indeed experiences of grace. They often occur early in a psychological process of religion and are initial encouragements, which sometimes drop away and are followed by long periods of spiritual dryness, even in great saints. These early sweets are not to be compared with the renewals of spiritual maturity in the higher mystics, though they convey the same message of God's love and peace to almost unformed souls. They have been so good to me that I am greatly thankful for them.

At the same period, one day when I was just about to have an afternoon nap in that bedroom, I had a very brief experience of a kind that I have never otherwise experienced. Momentarily I was walking on the left hand side behind a coffin in Camley Church, the church where my father was buried. The man in front of me was wearing a green greatcoat in a coarse heavy material I had never seen before; under my feet there was the crunch of straw or rushes as though I had been walking in a barn. I did not then know, but have since established, that in the eighteenth century it was still customary to spread rushes on the church floor.

These experiences, all of which are of types widely recorded, have little or no evidential value to anyone else, and I do not put them forward as evidence. They do however have great evidential value for me. If someone who has complete confidence in his senses, and knows himself to be in his right mind, finds that he has premonitory dreams which do in fact foretell, has a sudden glimpse into the past which is as real in physical detail as an experience of the present, and, above all, has sudden intimations of the spiritual harmony of life, he has no right to call on anyone else to be convinced, but he is very likely to be convinced himself. And of what will he be convinced? He will feel that the materialist explanation, which depends on the absolute character of time, cannot be true. He will tend to believe that the explanation of the universe is spiritual rather than material, and that is a large beginning.

In particular mortality is a concept which belongs to time; people are born in time, live in time and die in time, and without time the sequence of causes and effects which make up our world could not exist. But if time is not the ultimate reality, then there must be a point of view from which the dead have not yet even been born, a point of view from which immortality is inevitable, since there is no rule of time to determine mortality. If for a half second—as I have reason to believe but no one else does—I followed an eighteenth-century coffin, then I lived for that half second a century and a half before my own birth, and perhaps forty years before my great grandfather was born. If those days still exist, why should I suppose that I shall disappear from reality at the time when my own death comes?

These arguments had a great impact on me at the time, and they still have some weight with me, though less than they had. I have not greatly studied psychical research, and have the fear that much of it is inherently dangerous. There is certainly something very displeasing about the fringes of the occult cults, an atmosphere of depression and shabbiness. Yet I do believe that these chinks in the order of the world, which seem to me to be amply established in the literature, though mostly not susceptible to rigorous scientific proof (because not repeatable), can have a value in opening the mind. If they open the mind to God, they are a good providence. But though I believe they can be for good, I am sure that psychic phenomena can be used by both sides.

It was however partly because I became convinced that the

6

mechanistic explanation did not fit my experience of the world that I became more seriously interested in the study of religion. A journalist becomes accustomed to quick invasions of great subjects; I found that there was a literature of almost unlimited scope, a large part of which was now read only by a minority of specialists. I came across the letters of Evelyn Underhill while browsing in a Wells bookshop; I had always been interested in Sir Thomas More as an historic figure; I now for the first time read St. Augustine's Confessions and Pascal, and some English authors I had originally purchased as a collector of eighteenth-century literature. I also became interested, partly through Evelyn Underhill's work on mysticism, in the history of Jewish mysticism, and particularly in Hasidism. I read translations of Plato, and Dean Inge on Plotinus, and William James. I read the Bible with a greater sense of its meaning, though even now, heaven knows, only too inadequately.

This reading strongly created in me a conviction of the reality of religious experience which has not since left me, and is now rooted in my mind as fact, so rooted that I do not even regard it as belief, in any sense in which belief is less certain than knowledge. All the masterpieces of religious writing describe the same reality. This I believe also to be true of religions of which I have a quite inadequate knowledge, such as the great Eastern religions, but I know it to be true of the religions of the West.

It is true of the Old Testament and the New; it is true of the great prophets of Judaism and the great rabbis; it is true of Plato and the neo-Platonists; it is true of the Apostles, of St. Paul and St. John and the great Saints of the Christian Church; it is, I believe, true of Islam, and certainly true of Sufi mysticism; above all it is true of Jesus himself. No one seriously reading these writings can doubt that they are all teaching about the same thing, that they are recounting the same ultimate experience.

What they describe is indeed indescribable, in the same sense that one cannot look into the eye of the sun, and cannot therefore hold in one's mind the idea of the sun's light in anything approaching its full truth. But they all tell us of a spiritual reality which is perfect, which is loving and which enters men's hearts. They all speak of that reality not as a hypothesis, but as something deeply experienced in their own lives. Moreover they all convey in their own lives and personalities some further idea of what this reality is, and Jesus does so to a unique degree, so that meditation on Jesus, even apart from Christian belief about the divine nature of Jesus, seems the same thing as meditation on God.

One does not need, I think, to be a Christian to see the power of this cloud of witnesses. Jesus would of course have said 'the God of Moses is my God', and one could describe the impact of God on men of high mystical gifts from Jewish literature alone, just as from Christian literature alone, or perhaps, though with some limitation, from Platonic literature. Indeed the literature is so abundant, and its similarity is so striking, that it is like a great sea which gives the same water wherever a bucket is put into it.

This has for me the very highest value as evidence. It is like the pre-photographic evidence for the existence of Everest; everyone who had been to the Himalayas to have a look had seen Everest and brought back a similar report. Men of different nations and cultures in different ages, with different theological beliefs, have all given the same report of the existence and nature of God, and those not bad men, but including the most admired, the most trusted, the most serene, the most loved and loving of mankind.

These arguments did therefore, and still do, satisfy my mind. But at the same time I had the good fortune to have a marriage and a parish religious life which supported and nourished these ideas. In Somerset, one of the most beautiful counties in England, we live within two and a half miles of the Benedictine monastery of Downside, which serves several of our local parishes, including Midsomer Norton where we go to church. The monk who has for more than fifteen years been our Parish Priest, Dom Benet Innes O.S.B., has devoted to the care of his parish talents which could have accomplished almost anything. His success can even be measured in a growing congregation, now a rare thing, but also in the deepening and strengthening of the religious lives of his parishioners, and the provision of great spiritual comfort. It is the institutional church which brings these blessings, and the devotion of a priest to his religion and his Church.

There has also in these years been for me the blessing of marriage. The energy of religion increases because the love of God makes one love man more, and the love of man makes one love God; each brings an increase in the other. There are many advantages in the celibate life, including the opportunity of prayer, of avoidance of some worldly cares, and the opportunity to devote one's life wholly to God. The advantage of married life is that it provides one both with the support of being loved and the opportunity to love, and with good fortune plenty of people to love. Family life is not always easy, and failures in family life are the failures one regrets most, but to love one's wife or children is a prayer in itself. I know how much ordinary family love has in my case led to a strengthening of religious faith.

I am with all this not a man who pretends to be particularly good; I do not think of myself as a good man, but as a selfish one; certainly I am not a good Christian. As one gets older specific sins seem to become less frequent—I am not thinking of sex—but constitutional inadequacies more grave. Yet however badly and selfishly I lead my life, I can now say that it has become the life of an unquestioning believer. The love of God is the only thing that matters ultimately in life, that and the love of human beings which flows from it and flows back into it. That is the reason of life, the end of life, the happiness of life and the duty of life; it is what man is for. However inadequately any of us may live by that standard, that is the truth, and those who have even intermittent understanding of that truth are fortunate indeed.

2

'Love is the greatest thing that God can give us, for himself
is Love; and it is the greatest thing we can give to God,
for it will also give ourselves, and carry with it all that is
ours. The Apostle calls it, *the band of perfection*; it is the
Old, and it is the New, and it is the great Commandment,
and it is all the Commandments, for it is *the fulfilling of the
law*. It does the work of all other graces, without any in-
strument but its own immediate virtue.... It is a grace
that loves God for himself, and our Neighbours for God.
The consideration of God's goodness and bounty, the experience of those profitable and excellent emanations from
him, may be, and most commonly are, the first motive of
our Love: but when we are once entered, and have tasted
the goodness of God, we love the spring for its own excellency, passing from passion to reason, from thanking to
adoring, from sense to spirit, from considering our selves
to an union with God: and this is the image and little
representation of Heaven; it is beatitude, in pictures, or
rather the infancy and beginnings of glory.'
                              Jeremy Taylor. *Holy Living: Of Charity, or the
                              Love of God*. (1650)

WHEN ONE has read that passage one should pause, and if
possible read it again, for it sums up not only the central
doctrine of the Christian faith, but the central truth about the
religious nature of man. It is the message of the Gospels; it is
the message of Jesus; it is put with the most beautiful eloquence by St. Paul. It is the truth by which the saints were
changed and it is the truth for which martyrs died, but it is
also the great and general consolation of mankind.

We Christians, who have the example, the teaching and

the grace of Jesus, are uniquely fortunate, but we are not unique in this doctrine; the God of love is the God of the whole world. He is certainly the God of the Torah and of the Koran just as he is the God of the Gospels. Each great religion is entitled to claim for itself that it is the highest expression of the love of God to man, but the ground of all religion is to be found in God's love for man, and that is universal, not limited in time or place. We may think of the religions of the world as though they were the colours of the spectrum; the colours indicate the different refractions of the light, but the light itself is the pure white light of God. It is of course true that many religions or cults have been corrupted or are by their primitive character inadequate or inferior. The doctrine that all religions are equal is an absurdity. But the fact of religion has its root in man's experience of God's love and in his response to it.

How far can one properly describe this as a universal response? Obviously many modern people do not feel that they have experience of God's love. It is however the evidence of the major world religions, which are indeed closely linked to each other. Buddhism is a branch of Hinduism; Hinduism has been strongly influenced by Islam; Judaism, Christianity and Islam all worship the same God, and the Jewish holy books, being the earliest, have significance for all three. Even in Hinduism, the most ancient and the least defined of these religions, this central impulse is apparent.

'He who is one, who dispenses the inherent needs of all peoples and all times, who is in the beginning and the end of all things, may He unite us with the bonds of goodwill.'

That prayer comes from the Upanishads, that is from Hindu scripture dating from about 800 BC; it would be now a perfectly orthodox prayer for a Jew, a Christian, a Moslem or a Buddhist. So much so that it would not appear out of place in the holy books or liturgy of anyone of these religions.

Again one has to guard against confusing the great religions; they are not identical, and their differences are not merely of cultural importance. But in the modern world, in an age of lost or failing faith, it is the unity of the religious fact from which they all spring that needs to be emphasized. Religions differ (and to a Christian the truth of Jesus is a vital

11

difference) but they are all based on the same truth. As the Hindu teacher Sadu (1544–1603) said: 'the giving up of self-regard, the worship of God, the curing of all corruptions of mind and body, the cultivation of friendship for all creatures —that is the essence.' Sadu admittedly was an unusual Hindu; he came of Muslim stock and aimed to create a world religion based on the simple core of religious beliefs, but he has had a continuing influence on Hindu thought, and the belief he so defined does indeed underlie all religion.

Ours is only a phase of history, statistically at least the most bloody and terrible man has ever known, in which faith has become particularly difficult for great numbers, perhaps for a majority of people. If one believes in God, the power of God is so strongly apparent that the idea of the world losing its religion has no possible justification. It is like the idea that one could take a canoe and row up Niagara Falls; there is no power in the universe capable of opposing itself to the will, that is to the love, of the creator of the universe. Least of all does man have such power.

Yet for man the loss of his sense of the love of God is terrible. The love of God is part of the fabric of our civilization, the most important part, and once it is lost, no civilization of value can survive. The greater tragedy is that without God man cannot die in peace, but the lesser tragedy is that without God man cannot live in peace. Both his immortal and his mortal life depend upon it.

Jesus used the metaphor of Christians leavening the world, and in Hasidic Judaism there is the belief in the Zadik, the good man who justifies his community in the sight of God. The most one can hope for is a constant permeation of society by religious ideas and by religious men. The dry agnostic societies of the West or the brutally atheist societies of the East are alike in rejecting or trying to limit the influence of religion upon them.

Yet consider what has happened in the least religious societies of history. In Western history there have been great empires of power, Imperial Rome, Nazi Germany, Soviet Russia. There is a hideous similarity between their systems of value and between their actual practices. All have killed on an imperial scale, they are beasts insatiable for human blood. All have worshipped their rulers, Augustus, Hitler,

12

Lenin, Stalin. All have persecuted the Jews, partly because the Jews would not join in the worship of the idolized state. All have persecuted the Christians, and the greater the saints the more they have sought to destroy them. All have rejected the principle of love, the love of God and the love of man, and all have adhered to the principle of power. Stalin's question—'How many divisions has the Pope?'—sums up the philosophy of all of them, and incidentally shows how limited they are.

These are the most striking examples of the anti-religious state. One can of course see that there was also a better element in the Roman state; these states become more horrible as history goes on, and have fewer redeeming attributes. Yet the alternative to the love of God in society seems not to be a mere indifference, but a contradiction of the love of God, and the substitution of the love of power, the worship of the idols of power, the stupidity of force, and the lusts of cruelty. One should not forget that many of the early Christian martyrs were not killed because the Emperors disapproved of Christianity, though they did, but because the Roman crowd liked watching people being killed.

Not only therefore is the belief in the love of God the basis of all religions, it is the basis of any human society that will itself be fit for human beings to live in, which our society in the twentieth century, on the ebb tide of faith, barely is. That is not to say that all non-religious societies are as bad as the worst. They do all become grossly mis-shapen, but their cultural history varies and the degree to which they move from a non-religious to an anti-religious attitude varies also. Even an anti-religious society itself cannot wholly conceal God's love for man, but it can prejudice man's ability to receive and respond to that love.

It is perhaps one of the strangest evidences of the reality of man's psychological relationship to God that the great imperial societies block man's response to God's love by mimicking that relationship. The divinity accorded to the Roman Emperors, the hysterical worship of the Führer which was consciously and artfully organized or orchestrated by Hitler himself, the worship at Lenin's tomb, the adulation of Stalin at a time when he was murdering millions of Russians, the worship of Mao Tse-Tung by the Chinese people,

13

all show the same phenomenon. The worship that it is natural for man to feel for God is diverted onto a human ruler.

This process has been well understood both by the Jewish and Christian religions. Unless one understands the threat of this substitution for God, one will not understand the emphasis of the Old Testament on the evil of idolatry, or the repeated warnings of Jesus that there will be many anti-Christs, that is false Messiahs. The most evil and destructive societies of the twentieth century have all been idolatrous, and evil in approximate proportion to their idolatry. The heroic leaders who have been made idols have offered a pseudo-religious satisfaction to their followers.

The great religions of the world would not have come into existence, or survived so many different and successive political institutions, if they had not corresponded to a need in man's mind. The pseudo-religious and idolatrous state systems, which never last very long, would not have their great but historically brief power, if they also did not meet a human psychological need. Their power comes from the mind of man: the Chinese would not worship Mao Tse-Tung if they had not been born with a faculty for worship, as all men are. Idols confirm the importance of the role of the religion which they mimic.

In essence this religious faculty in man consists of 'the giving up of self-regard, the worship of God' and the love of God. The only remotely plausible non-religious explanation of the origin of this psychological function in man is that God is a father-substitute. But is this what babies feel for their fathers? Apart from the fact that small babies are much more conscious of their mothers, babies are not altruistic and indeed nature could not afford them to be altruistic. One can see that babies might worship their fathers, as powerful external beings, but is it plausible that this worship should lend to 'the giving up of self regard'? In any case the emotions are disproportionate. The unlimited power of the love of God, as seen in the lives of the saints, is quite unlike the strong but natural effects of love inside a family.

If we accept that religion fills a need for a loving relationship with a being not ourselves, which the great religions all meet, and the great anti-religions also meet but in a distorted and defective way, then we have to consider whether the

14

meeting of this need is good for man. Obviously religions suffer from the corruptions of humanity; religion can be a cloak or an excuse for all sorts of evils. There is indeed a danger that religion will inflate the spirit; that is the point of the parable of the Publican and the Pharisee; but the pride of the Pharisee is a denial of the central doctrine of Christianity. If a man believes that he is loved by and loves an all-powerful God, and has a relationship with God, that in itself tends to create patterns of love in his own psychology and in his social attitudes.

The experience of piety bears this out. We have all met really good men, men full of love for mankind, largely free of concern for themselves and marked with the peace which the shedding of human cares and a sense of the presence of God can give. We can read books which have this authentic sense of peace and love for mankind. The supreme example for me, as it has been for so many, is St. John's Gospel; the picture of Jesus drawn in that Gospel is something which the whole of the rest of the world's experience of religion, Christian and non-Christian, never seems quite to reach.

The authentic tone of peace and love, of joy and hope, of faith in a benevolent order of the world, is not confined to Christianity, but it is a universal occurrence in human history. Yet these qualities of love and unselfishness are seen as good not only by religious people. Atheists would accept that a man full of love, and enjoying peace of mind, is better than a man full of hate, whose mind is in a turmoil of self-regard and self-seeking. One does not have to be a Christian to see that it is better to be St. Francis of Assisi than, say, to be Dr. Goebbels.

We have therefore a characteristic of the human mind which, while not strongly found in all men, is present in large numbers of men in all ages and countries of which we have knowledge. It changes the lives of those who possess it, and is admired by those who do not. It cannot be explained in any convincing way as merely an adjunct of infantile psychology or the struggle for survival (true religion might be expected, as Hitler would have argued, to weaken warrior tribes in their struggle to survive). It is moreover benevolent. It makes men better, even when one applies the standards of those who do not accept it.

This argument falls short of proof that religion is true, but it does have some awkward questions to be answered by those who assert that the ground of religion is false. If it is false, how did man come to have this hunger for it? If it is false, how does it come to be so strong in its influence on man? If it is false, how does it come to be so good for man? The existence of this hunger for God, the strength of this love of God, the benefit to human nature of faith in God cannot be denied without denying the evidence of the whole of human history.

The argument that is left is that this is a benign illusion which has somehow, no-one can say precisely how, come to be developed by a process of natural selection in the mind of man. I find it very hard to bring myself to believe in benign illusions: my experience of error is that, however attractive it looks at first sight, it invariably proves harmful and damaging before very long. That is certainly true of error in practical human affairs, in political life; how should it not be true in matters of religion? I could understand, except that it is obviously untrue, the argument that God is a non-existent being whom it is bad for us to believe in. What I cannot accept is the argument that God is a non-existent being whom it is good for us to believe in.

This is all the more difficult to believe when one considers the abundant Christian literature on the lives of the saints. Saints are not supernatural beings; they are ordinary human beings who have had all kinds of human temperament, and all kinds of human experiences as their background. They have often been people with great natural difficulties of personality to overcome; indeed that is so far true that there seem to be more saints who start with stronger but rather unpleasant characters than they are who start with weaker but sweeter natures. Anyone can become a saint, and kings and beggars, soldiers and businessmen, abbesses and sewing girls have all done so.

It is the development of sanctity in the soul which is so fascinating, and it is difficult to parallel in any psychological process which is neither religious nor quasi-religious. In many cases there is a moment of conversion, sudden, total and often ecstatic, like the conversion of St. Paul on the road to Damascus. At one point there is the old, self-regarding personality; a moment later, as though by a miracle, and presumably in fact by a miracle, there is the Christian personality, personality turned inside out so that the love and concern for self becomes love and concern for others. These conversions are particularly notable in the history of Methodism.

More often there is a gradual process by which the characteristics of the old personality are shed and the characteristics of the new are acquired. I find this gradual and natural process, a sort of flowering of the soul, the more moving of the two. Such a development one finds in Sir Thomas More, and, very beautifully documented, in the life of Cardinal Newman. The spiritual life of Pope John was of this gradually flowering kind.

One sees, as the decades pass, the personality of the saint being more and more completely penetrated with Christian grace, until at the end all can see the complete disinterestedness, the dropping away of all the cocoon of worldly nature, of the last shadows of self-seeking. To care nothing for oneself, to care everything for others, to live for and in the presence of God, is the achievement of the last stages of the lives of the greatest Saints; it is, as Jeremy Taylor, himself a Bishop of the English Church and a man of the highest holiness, calls it, a 'little representation of heaven'.

Of course the lives of the saints have sometimes been written in a way that is sentimental and exaggerated, but the character of this spiritual development is so well authenticated in so many cases (and indeed in holy men of all the religions) that it cannot be doubted by anyone who is prepared to face the facts of religion. Certainly the devotees of good and bad non-religious causes are capable of remarkable self-sacrifice for their causes, but in the career of the non-religious zealots one does not find a similar psychological development, a similar sanctification. Che Guevara has been perhaps the most admired Communist devotee of modern times, and Pope John perhaps the most moving Christian leader since the war. The story of Pope John is one of sanctification and universal love; the story of Che Guevara is, on the most favourable view, nothing like that.

The strongest evidence of the truth of God's love, of the existence of God and the existence of his love, is not to be found in philosophy but in the working of God's love that can be seen in the lives of men. Not all good men are religious but

17

there is this large group of men, of whom examples can be found in all ages and all countries and all religions. They show a freedom from the normal selfishness of life and a capacity for love which human nature only shows at its highest. They all say, in different theological terms, that they have received the blessing of this freedom as a gift from God, and they make it their most earnest business to try to spread this knowledge of God to their fellow men. If they are all mistaken and God is a mere fiction, then we have to accept that the greatest and best men the human race has ever produced, the men of love who stand so much higher than the men of power, were all developed by the same reliance on the same mistake.

It would be a similar proposition if it were argued that not only Mozart, but almost all the greatest composers and almost all the greatest musicians the world had ever known, were only great musicians by a common and happy error, and that had they really understood the truth about music they would not have been able to compose at all.

Such propositions are not absolutely inconceivable, but they are extremely unlikely. The difficulty of the atheists's position is that he cannot undo the miracles of God. The miracles of spiritual sanctification of human lives occurred, and are still occurring. Is it plausible that these miracles were performed not by God, but by a false belief in a God who does not exist? Plainly Pope John was a greater man than the plump Italian lawyer he might have become if he had lost his faith; if God does not exist, that plump Italian lawyer eating his spaghetti would have had the truth, and the great Pope and Saint would have owed his greatness to his failure to see where the truth lay. He would have received the gift of loving the whole world from a non-existent being about whom he had mistaken beliefs. What a strange false God it would be who gives real grace.

The paradox of atheism is therefore far greater, and far harder to believe, than any of the paradoxes of religion. We see in the saints men who have been set free. We believe that it is the truth which set them free, but atheists have to believe that the saints were set free by a lie, while agnostics believe that the saints were set free by a hypothesis which may or may not be correct.

18

3

'No man that knoweth the perfections of God, will ever believe that he would bless a deceiver, and a lie, to be the means of the most holy and excellent work that ever was done in the world.'

Richard Baxter. *The Reasons of the Christian Religion.* (1667)

ALL MEN who are brought to Christian belief are brought by the Holy Ghost. Yet some seem to come to belief in Jesus Christ from belief in God the Father, and others come to belief in God because they have a direct belief in Jesus Christ.

Most people who come to Christian belief have the experience first of a childhood belief, followed by a period of doubts in adolescence or after adolescence, leading again to a matured adult belief when they have thought through their faith. Certainly I went through this process, which makes faith something like a figure of eight, with a narrow place in the middle in which it is almost constricted. Richard Baxter, the seventeenth-century Presbyterian divine, describes it in his own life:

'The last sort of religion to be enquired into, is CHRIS-TIANITY: in which by the Providence of God I was educated, and at first received it by a humane faith, upon the word and reverence of my parents and teachers, being unable in my childhood rationally to try its grounds and evidences.

'In this Religion (received defectively both as to matter and grounds) I found a power even in my childhood, to awe my soul, and check my sin and folly, and make me careful of my salvation, and to make me love and honour true wisdom and holiness of life.

'But when I grew up to fuller use of reason, and more fully

19

understood what I had generally and darkly received, the power of it did more surprize my mind, and bring me to deeper consideration of spiritual and everlasting things: it humbled me in the sense of my sin and its deserts: and made me think more sensibly of a Saviour: it resolved me for more exact obedience to God: and increased my love to God: and increased my love to persons and things, sermons, writings, prayers, conference, which relished of plain resolved Godliness. . . .

'At last having for many years laboured to compose my mind and life, to the principles of this Religion, I grew up to see more difficulties in it, than I saw before: And partly by temptations, and partly by an inquisitive mind, which was wounded with uncertainties and could not contemptuously or carelessly cast off the doubts which I was not able to resolve, I resumed afresh the whole enquiry, and resolved to make as faithful a search into the nature and grounds of this Religion, as if I had never been baptized into it.'

Such a process of childish faith, doubt and mature faith must be regarded as so normal that one cannot know whether somebody who has never known doubt is very fortunate, as some undoubtedly are, to have a faith of exceptional vigour from the beginning, or has missed an almost necessary stage of spiritual and psychological development. Unfortunately many, and particularly many nowadays, are shipwrecked in their doubts, often being overwhelmed by real difficulties, but also often being defeated by difficulties which could easily have been set aside.

I certainly found myself at one point wholly convinced of the existence and love of God, and of God as described in the Old and the New Testaments (leaving aside some of the more angry moments in the Old Testament), but had no comparable faith in Jesus. The difficulty is again put very well and precisely by Baxter, though rather more flatteringly than my then state of mind would probably have deserved.

'That a man appearing like one of us, is the eternal word of God incarnate, is a thing which no man is bound to believe, without very sound evidence to prove it. God hath made reason essential to our nature; it is not our *weakness*, but our natural excellency, and his image on our natures.

Therefore he never called on us to renounce it, and to lay it by.'

The argument that in practice convinced me of the truth of the claim of Christ was based on the Lord's Prayer. The argument that came to me was this. I believe in God; the Lord's Prayer is a perfect expression of man's relationship to God, a prayer which has been the focus of the spiritual lives of hundreds of millions of Christians; if Jesus saw man's relationship to God so simply and so clearly that he could give us this prayer, he will not have been mistaken about his own relationship to God.

That argument still seems to me to be good, though simple. If one reads the lives and writings of other holy men one cannot find the equal, or even the approximate equal, of Jesus. I would exempt from this generalization the character of Buddha, not because I believe Buddha to be an equal figure, but because I do not know enough about Buddhism for any judgment to be proper. With that exception, or hypothetical exception, Jesus seems to me to be at the least the transcendent spiritual genius of the human race.

If one takes the greatest Christian saints, or the greatest philosophers, or the great men of the Old Testament, or the holy men of other religions, they none of them seem to me to approach the spiritual quality of Jesus. It is not, as it is with the arts, a case of there being a few men of genius, all about equal though immeasurably superior to the rest of us. It is a case of there being one single instance of a quality at least as much superior to the highest genius, as that genius is superior to the ordinary level. And of course one comes to believe that the distance is much greater than that.

The anti-Christian theist—the man who believes in God but not in Jesus—is therefore involved in the same difficulty as the atheist. The atheist has to believe in the existence of a benign error; it is apparent that the fruits of religious belief include peace and love and humility and that these are the highest and most valuable qualities in human nature. The atheist has to believe that men acquire these virtues, as in religion they undoubtedly do acquire them, by believing in a lie.

The anti-Christian has to take this further. The life and

21

work of Jesus has, at the lowest claim, resulted in religion in one of its most noble forms being spread widely through the world. Jesus himself, again putting it at the lowest, is a spiritual teacher and leader of the highest genius, and a man filled with the spirit of love. Yet if we do not accept his claims for himself we are saying that this work, which Baxter rightly calls the work of sanctification, is in this case also achieved by a lie. Jesus himself gave as his test of the truth of religious claims 'by their fruits shall ye know them.' Of course the Christian religion, like all human institutions, has its corruptions, evils the more powerful as they have some of the energy of religion, but can one believe that two thousand years of sanctity have sprung from a root of falsehood?

I think some people's difficulties, and I found it so in my own case, spring from looking for religious truth in the creeds rather than in the Gospels. If we recite the Nicene, or still more the Athanasian, creed we can if we are not careful start a wholy covey of theological doubts. The creeds need to be seen in their historic context.

The early church had the message of Christ and the teaching of the Apostles, but it had to develop a series of concepts and definitions which would protect the teaching of the Church from error. This process resulted in a great deal of controversy, much of it more acrimonious than it should have been, and the advocacy of numerous heresies, that is of false doctrines capable of doing serious damage to the truth of Christian belief and to the influence of Christianity on human life.

In order to guard against these heresies various Councils of the Church had to make definitions of doctrine, both on particular points and on belief as a whole. This development of the Church's understanding of its own faith has continued to the present day, but the ferment of ideas was naturally at its greatest in the early centuries.

The creeds are therefore precise theological statements designed to prevent the Church and its members from falling into error, and the definitions are influenced, necessarily, by the errors they are designed to exclude. They were not only intended, and in particular the Athanasian creed was not intended, to be a summary of necessary beliefs for ordinary Christians, but to be a series of definitions designed to exclude heresies which are now largely forgotten, though no heresy seems ever wholly to die. When the Athanasian creed says: 'as also there are not three incomprehensibles, nor three uncreated: but one uncreated, and one incomprehensible,' we should neither disbelieve it, for it is one tiny part of the mosaic of the infallible teaching of the Church, nor worry about it if we cannot understand it. Its purpose is to guard the Church against error; its language is that of the theological draftsman excluding a misinterpretation, not of a teacher, not of Jesus himself. It bears the same relationship to good Christian living as the language of a statute does to good citizenship.

We shall not after all be mistaken if we follow Jesus himself. It is in St. John's Gospel that the clearest statements of what he saw as his relationship with God the Father are to be found. 'As my father hath taught me, I speak these things. And he that hath sent me is with me: the Father hath not left me alone; for I do always those things that please him. . . . Before Abraham was, I am. . . . I am the good shepherd, and know my sheep and am known of mine. As the Father knoweth me, even so I know the Father: and I lay down my life for the sheep. . . . I and my Father are one. . . . If I do not the works of my Father believe me not. But if I do, though ye believe not me, believe the works: that ye may know and believe, that the Father is in me, and I in him.'

For many people, it seems to me, the difficulty lies not in the fact of the Trinity, but in the formulation. If he tries to understand what the Athanasian creed means, an ordinary layman is immediately in considerable difficulty; perhaps even a trained theologian is in some difficulty. Yet when one gets back to the words which Jesus actually used, 'the Father is in me, and I in him,' the difficulty drops away. I find no difficulty, in however complete a metaphysical sense, in believing Jesus' statement that 'I and my Father are one.'

I have indeed no wish to reduce the doctrines of the church in order to make them more palatable. On the contrary I believe the truths of the universe to be infinitely more mysterious and astonishing than the human mind could possibly conceive. But I do feel it is a mistake for people to be too preoccupied with reading the title deeds when they should be living in the house. Religion is the reality; definitions are a necessary but limited way of looking at that reality.

The strongest proof of the claims of Jesus seem to me to be found in the Gospels and in the lives of those who have followed his religion. The Gospels each of us must read for ourselves. I am much struck by their Jewish character, and feel the greatest thankfulness to Judaism for having been the setting and home for the life of Jesus. Mary, the Mother of God, was a Jewish mother; what could honour a people compared to that? Jesus was a Jew, and in many ways an orthodox one. The life of Jesus reinforces for me, as it must have done for the first Christians, the sense of the presence of God in the Torah.

There is some danger in allowing oneself too personal a view of the human character of Jesus. Those who have written lives of him have given very different accounts of what they thought his personality to be. There is in any case a difference of emphasis in different Gospels. Yet when that is said, his personality is still the most powerful inducement to religion that there is.

Above all, the sacrifice that Jesus made, which Christians believe was made for us, was made with such love, including love for those who persecuted him, that the crucifixion reveals a personality which has inspired all Christians since that time. The early Christians believed because of the miracle of the resurrection, but the miracle lies in the acceptance of the crucifixion as well.

Yet the proof that is derived from the effect of Jesus in human history is perhaps equally convincing, for it continues to the present day. Let me take just two examples. In *The Times* of February 20th, 1976, Mr. Bernard Levin quotes a poem written by Georgi Vins, a Russian Baptist pastor from Kiev. He served in a concentration camp from 1966 to 1969; he is at present, if still alive, again in a concentration camp. His father died in a Soviet concentration camp in 1943; all for the offence of being Christians.

My persecutors, I do not curse you,
And at this hour under the burden of the cross
I pray for you and bless you
With the simple humanity of Christ.
I am pure before you: by my words and deeds
I have called you to good and to light.

I have so much wished that your hearts
Would be possessed by the lofty ideal of Love.
But rejecting this kind summons
You answered with rabid enmity.
My persecutors, I do not curse you,
But I am saddened by your fate.

It is of course true that many causes, even many bad causes, have had their martyrs. It is much more rare for martyrs to die in charity towards their persecutors, and I have read of no instance of a martyr to a bad cause dying in charity to his executioners. Such charity is not unknown among good men outside Christianity—indeed it is true of Socrates—but it is extremely rare. In Christianity it is the consistent witness of nearly two thousand years, starting with the Crucifixion itself.

The other example is taken from Fleury's *History of the Church*; Fleury is relying on the historian Eusebius; the persecution is that of the Emperor Marcus Aurelius, the most philosophical of the Roman Emperors—there is something particularly odious about persecution by a professional philosopher.

'Under these circumstances the Martyrs displayed their humility and charity; and so greatly did they desire to imitate Jesus Christ, that after having confessed his name, not only once or twice but several times, after having been exposed to wild beasts, burnt and covered with wounds, they assumed not to themselves the title of Martyrs, and would not permit us to honour them with that title; but if any of us called them Martyrs, either in writing or speaking of them, they greatly complained of it. . . . They were filled with the fear of God, and humbled themselves under his mighty hand; excusing everybody, accusing none, and praying for those who evil entreated them.'

Perhaps some people think it is easy to be a martyr; I am very sure it is not. It is the most extreme proof of faith, and yet the Christian martyrs in 177 A.D. or 1976 A.D. show exactly the same spirit, and it is the spirit of forgiveness and charity of Jesus himself. Again one has to ask oneself whether this can come from a lie, whether for so many centuries a lie could lead to conduct of such rarely paralleled humility, courage and love.

Is it not also true that the persecutors give evidence in their own way? The witness of the Christians has to be given against the evil of power, and it is clear from history that bad men feel a strong urge to crush and to destroy Christianity. If religion were not true, if Chistianity were not the most highly developed truth of all religion, what need would there be for it to be persecuted in this way? There is probably now no dictatorship in the world which does not have Christians in its prisons because of their Christian witness, as they are in the prisons of Russia and South Africa and Chile. The persecutors realize the threat that Christianity must always be to them. In the same way the endless persecutions of the Jews reflect the resentment of evil men at the strength and truth, not the falsehood, of Jewish belief.

It is not however only the lives of the martyrs which gives the decisive evidence of the truth of Christ. We are all, as I said, converted by the Holy Ghost; it is certain also that we are also all converted, if we are converted, by other Christians, by the prayers of other Christians, perhaps unknown to us, and particularly by the example of Christian lives, often lives of no heroic quality, but of 'plain resolved Godliness.'

If it is a man's experience, and it has been mine, that Christianity truly accepted generally tends to make people better than they could otherwise be expected to be, not only in their actions but in their souls, and in the wholeness and health of their personalities, that in itself must be strong evidence that Christ does work in them. It is what one would expect if Christianity was true, that not only the saints and martyrs, but ordinary people would be better for it, more compassionate, better able to love their fellows, more at peace with themselves, more confident for the future, asking less of the present. It is what one would expect, and in my experience it is so.

Nor, I believe, is this a matter of doctrine. I do not think that people are good because they have read instructions to be good. I believe that they become good because their souls have been penetrated with the goodness of God, because the Holy Spirit is in them, with the love of the Father and the example and redemptive sacrifice of the Son. I do not believe that people in this important way become good for purely natural reasons, but that they become better for supernatural reasons. They have a relationship with God by which they are changed, and acquire at least some of the supernatural longings which are the normal response to a sense of God's love.

In this psychology of spiritual development Christ is all important. He is the example; he is the founder of our religion; he is the presence of God on earth; he is the teacher; he is the redeemer and sacrifice; he is the resurrection; but above all he is the author of the religion which teaches love of God, love of man and disregard of self, a religion which proves to be true to the deepest requirements of human nature, and relieves man of the agonies of his own false ambitions. Without the mediating figure of Jesus not one in a thousand of those who have through Christianity come to a true understanding of religion would have been able to do so.

It is these gifts which are so great, and so strongly supported by grace, by prayer and by Holy Communion, which must either come from the truth or prove a lie. It is natural that Christians should believe that it is the truth which sets us free. It is also much more reasonable than the supposition that we owe joy and salvation and humility and peace to what could at best be a ridiculous misunderstanding.

4

It must be confessed that of Christ, working as a creator, and a governor of the world by providence, all are partakers; not all partakers of that grace, whereby he inhabiteth whom he saveth. Again as he dwelleth not by grace in all, so neither doth he equally work in all them in whom he dwelleth. *Whence it is* (saith St. Augustine) *that some be holier than others are, but because God doth dwell in some more plentifully than in others.*

Richard Hooker. *Ecclesiastical Polity Book V.* (1597)

THE QUESTION which St. Augustine raises, which also concerned Hooker, is one of the most puzzling in religion. Anyone who believes in religion at all comes to see it as far the most important matter in life, an eternal matter in a temporal world. Yet not only grace, but that particular grace which consists of a natural sense of religion, seems to be very unevenly distributed.

It is certainly the case that some people have their minds open to religion in a way others do not. There are people, often leading quite worldly lives, who feel themselves always to be in the presence of God, as indeed they are. Equally there are people, often those leading dutiful lives, for whom the idea of God means nothing, who have no inkling that there could be a spiritual reality not to be perceived by their physical senses. As with most gifts the majority, of course, lie between these two extremes.

This variation in spiritual sensibility, in the talent for sensing spiritual facts, is so well attested that it does not seem to require argument. It should be a warning to those who because they have no inkling of even the possibility of spiritual truth believe that no one else has either. Yet how unfair it seems to be. One may compare it to the sense of music; some people have perfect pitch, most are fairly musical, some are tone deaf. Yet for the religious sense to be distributed as unevenly as the musical sense, and apparently as arbitrarily, does seem to be unfair; religion is after all a much more important matter than music.

No doubt in the end God gives grace to every soul, but it is certain that in this world, and in our extremely limited experience, the distribution is very uneven. It is also uneven as between different countries and different ages of history, though perhaps not as uneven as we think. In what period and in what place can a real age of faith be located? So far as my reading of history goes, there has always been a pious minority, and they always have been a minority. The majority have always been decent folk, ordinary people of kindly human dispositions but not very religious. There has also always been a minority of evil men who have always hated God and religion and worshipped power, and have sometimes through winning power been able to control the lives of whole nations. This is the pattern even of our present age of unfaith, though undoubtedly the non-religious majority are more remote from religion than they have normally been in the past, and the evil men are, or in the earlier twentieth century have been, unusually prominent and powerful.

If one could plot the religious faculty on a graph it would, I am almost sure, appear as the familiar bell-shaped graph which reflects the distribution of most natural faculties. It is well established that height is distributed in this way; there are a few giants and only a few more very tall people; there are a few very short people and even fewer midgets; the great majority cluster closely round the average heights for men and women. Religion seems to show the same distribution, with a small group of deeply religious, a small group of anti-religious and a majority of mildly religious or not very religious. The measurement can also be applied in a similar way to good and evil; a few are very good, a few very evil; the majority are of a middling and mild moral quality. While religion aids virtue, some people are good beyond their sense of religion, and some are very religious, and genuinely so, but weak.

This is the division that observation would suggest. It

corresponds both with the Catholic church's traditional distinction between a state of grace and a state of mortal sin, and more precisely with the distinction in theology between the natural man and the sanctified or Christian soul. It also corresponds to the Catholic doctrine about the next world.

There are in Catholic teaching four abodes of departed souls, in descending order, heaven, purgatory, limbo and hell. Limbo is the place of rest of uninformed but virtuous souls— it is traditionally the place of unbaptized infants. It is a place of natural but not supernatural happiness.

This seems to correspond to the experience we have of people on earth. There is the highest experience of mystical prayer, not continuous even in the case of the greatest mystical saints. It is called the unitive state, and experience of it— including apparently generous experience of it—is not peculiar to the Christian religion. That is almost an experience of heaven while still on earth—but it is an exceptionally rare spiritual gift, the crown of a lifetime of devotion.

The ordinary states of soul seem to fall into three categories. The first is the state of a very good man, the state of the Saints; it is still a reaching towards and preparation for heaven, and therefore should be likened to purgatory rather than to heaven itself. It is still a time of testing and a time when the grosser appetites and selfishness of human nature are being purged away, but have not yet disappeared. It is however a state of mind of love and prayer and of direction of the will towards God. That is the state of grace in its fullest sense.

Then there is the natural state, neither very good nor very bad, neither very religious, nor very irreligious. It is the state of soul, if he will allow me the comparison, that is normally played by Mr. Kenneth More in his films. It is the spiritual state of what used to be called the good fellow or the decent chap. The natural life, because man is made in the image of God and because God's grace is universal, tends to good; at its best it shades off into the life of sanctity, but it is not an active religious life, and viewed from the point of view of man's possible relationship with God it represents an unconscious self-deprivation of happiness.

At its worst, and the natural state has necessarily a wide range, it shades off into the life of evil. The life of evil is what is really meant by mortal sin, a rage and hatred against God —a terrible religion of its own with the great blasphemous commandment—hate God and hate thy neighbour as thyself.

Modern man is very bad at facing the existence of evil, which is odd because the modern age has had such extensive experience of it. Yet, while we should hesitate to diagnose mortal sin in anyone but ourselves, it is evident that there is a spiritual condition in which the soul has gone over to the opposition. One may talk of the devil, or merely consider the condition as one of exclusion of God from the soul as an act of will, like a fortress shutting out the offer of peace.

Certainly there is in evil a particular emptiness of feeling. In this century we have had, in Hitler and Stalin, two of the great geniuses of evil; the devil's saints have in our unfortunate century had more genius than the saints of God. Yet when one thinks about Hitler or Stalin one comes to feel that they are not whole people, but empty, and emotional cripples. Inside them there seems to be nothing, not an 'I am', but an 'I am not' of personality. It is not only that Christ is not in them, but that nothing is in them, like a nut which has been eaten out by a worm, inside an unbroken shell.

Yet there does seem to be more to it than this. Apart from the mere absence of God, there seems in human history to be a lust for evil, a desire to destroy and deface, which goes beyond anything that self-interest would suggest and perhaps goes beyond the animal conditioning of man. The state of evil, of mortal sin, has in it a great deal which can be accounted for by its being merely a deprivation of good, but something in it which suggests, as the practices of black magic and some primitive rituals suggest, the worship of spiritual forces of evil.

If one accepts this division into four spiritual conditions, the unitive state, the sanctified state, the natural state and the state of mortal sin, of heaven, purgatory, limbo and hell, one is putting together concepts which have authority for them, but putting them together in a speculative way. One is also in obvious danger of making categories which run into each other appear to be sharply definite and distinct.

Yet this speculation, which does not seem to go against the orthodox view, gives a pattern to life which I find interesting and plausible. One of the objections sometimes made to traditional Christian teaching is that it appears to simplify life into a sort of pass or fail examination, in which those who just obtain a pass mark will go to heaven, for all eternity, while those who just fail will go to hell, also for eternity. No one would believe that such a system was either just or benevolent, and it does therefore contradict our notions of a just and benevolent God.

Yet if one tries to argue the whole thing away, and destroy the concept of hell, for humanitarian reasons, one comes up against two problems. One is the fact of evil; the other is the doctrine of the church. If there is no hell, then what happens to evil souls?—if there is no hell, then the church has been in error and so has the New Testament.

I would see the process as being one of education rather than examination; I hope and trust that all the people I know will be saved because I see that life touches them with an experience of truth that tends towards heaven. But I accept also that they have free will. If they choose they can swim the other way, and some people do swim the other way. I am not sure that there can be salvation against a man's will, and if there cannot then some will make a hell for themselves, if not eternally then for so long as they hold out against God.

Perhaps this process will at some stage be accelerated by the day of judgement, but the learning process has, I believe, to take place anyway. We have to learn to love God and to give up ourselves for that love; there is nothing else for it but to learn that lesson. Until we have learned it we shall not be ready for heaven; it is not that God would not be delighted to have us there, but we would have no place there, we would not fit. I know how far I am from having learned that lesson myself, and I see how far from having learned it are all the people about me. I believe and hope and trust that they and I will be given the grace to begin and to complete the learning of that lesson, and believe that in some degree we have begun it. But until we have learned it I do not see what we can expect but the purgatory of worldliness in this life, and the blessed purgatory of preparing to go to heaven in the next.

If there are any people, and I think that such do exist, who have a clear will to reject God and to exalt themselves, then it seems inevitable that they will make a hell for themselves and something like a hell for others in this life. It is not possible to be selfish without being both unhappy and destructive (as we all know from our experience of our own selfishness) and it is not possible to be totally selfish without being extremely unhappy and destructive. Some of this selfishness may be sickness of mind for which the will is not responsible, or not fully responsible, but if the soul goes into the next world wilfully and knowingly worshipping itself and hating God, shouting 'I, I, I' like a rich man in a queue, then the next world will be a very unhappy place for that soul. I do not see how it can be otherwise.

Do we know that such souls will ever repent? We do not know whether they will or whether they will not. We do know that God's love for them is not only equal to his love for the rest of us, but if anything greater, for they are his lost sheep. God even loves secret policemen. We do know that his mercy is infinite. But we may believe that in making man in his own image God endowed him with a capacity of free will which is not finite in quality, that can in theory hold out against unlimited grace for an unlimited time. We can only regard that as a mystery. But a mystery makes more sense than a contradiction, and it would be a contradiction for souls which hate God to be sent conscript to heaven. For one thing, they could not possibly be happy there.

It is because this is a process of learning that differences in grace, in the knowledge of Christ, are not unfair in the way that they would otherwise seem to be. The reaction of our own wills must make a difference to the process of learning, but the differences that make some holier than others may in the end prove to be differences in the stage of a learning process, rather than absolute differences in the graces given.

It is not unfair in school that boys in the sixth form have been educated beyond the stage of boys in the first; we have also the assurance of Jesus that all the labourers in the vineyard shall be paid equally at the end of the day.

I do not believe in reincarnation, because I do not believe two human beings could ever be identical, but this seems to be part, and perhaps the true part, of the Hindu doctrine of reincarnation, in which many lives are spent on the way to perfection. The idea of a ladder of spiritual progress is of course also found in Judaism and in Islam. Spiritual advancement is the natural interpretation of Jacob's ladder; it is

33

sometimes interpreted in a mystical sense and sometimes in a simpler sense of progress in piety. The Greater Hekhalot describes the pious man as one who has 'a ladder in his house'. In the Koran Allah is called 'the Lord of the Stairways' and Muhammad's night journey ended by his ascension from the site of the Temple in Jerusalem by means of a ladder of great beauty to the seventh heaven and into the presence of God.*

That this life should be treated as part of a ladder of spiritual schooling which may have begun with the grace of Baptism and may be completed in the graces of purgatory is a legitimate view for Christians, and it makes the religious function of life one of the education of a soul rather than the achievement of a specific degree of sanctification, which may or may not be inside our reach. We should none of us be surprised that we are not yet perfect.

The essence of the education of a soul is to turn from the selfishness of the natural man, away from the heightened selfishness of self-conscious evil, away from the worship of self and the worship of power, toward abnegation and unselfishness, and to the love of others; in St Paul's terms we pass from the first Adam to the last Adam, from 'a living soul' to 'a quickening spirit'. This education has to go extremely deep. Not only is human nature in fact very selfish, it has had to be. No doubt in terms of Darwinism certain kinds of family love, particularly mother love, and social loyalty—say the team work of hunters—have helped man to survive. But the flint-like determination to survive oneself, which underlies the most gentle characters, must have been the consistent requirement of the organism if it were to survive even the pre-human phase of evolution. We are as selfish as sharks and for the same motives of survival.

The evangelical clergymen of the eighteenth and nineteenth centuries, including the Wesleys, used to preach that unregenerate man had to be changed, had to be born again. I have argued they put too much emphasis on sudden conversion and too little on gradual spiritual enlightenment, but their estimate of the nature and degree of the change was fully justified. Man has to put off 'the old Adam', that is his evolutionary character, and 'put on Christ', that is a character of

* *The Ladder of Ascension* is discussed in Professor Altmann's *Studies in religious philosophy and mysticism*. Routledge and Kegan Paul, 1969.

self-sacrifice and love for others. That is surely right; it is exactly what any Christian has to do, at some stage in his spiritual education. It may sometimes be done in a moment, though even so the moment has usually been well prepared, but more often it is the work of a lifetime, or, I think, of a lifetime and of purgatory as well.

We can therefore see the outlines of Christian psychology. The basic change in the soul is from love of self, inevitable in the natural man, to love of others and love of God. The process is usually a gradual and educational one, though, like other educational processes, marked by sudden jumps in understanding. It is the process described in the Rule of St. Benedict as making 'ever more and more progress toward God.' This change takes the soul from the decent but selfish morality of the natural man to a love of God which finds its expression in the purest and highest acts of worship of God and love for man; indeed it takes the soul to the gates of heaven. If the process fails, as it sometimes does, inevitably the natural man reappears, but if it is reversed by a wilful and angry rejection of God, a hatred of God, it can move the soul to a state of evil not part of natural man or normal to him. At the very extreme the process of sanctification can lead to the unitive state in which man has virtually direct experience of God while still alive—this is seen only by the greatest saints and mystics.

This Christian psychology seems to me to make sense of the problem as St. Augustine states it, which is otherwise a bewildering one. It also provides a psychology of betterment, in a way that no alternative psychological theory can offer. If the fruits of holiness are peace, joy and love, how do we achieve these obviously desirable states of mind? Modern analytical psychology may help to correct some gross psychological disorders; those who have been through the hands of psychologists may at best emerge mended; those who have been through the hands of God emerge transformed, and made whole.

What is the mechanism of this process of Christian education? It is one of grace and it is one of relationship. I have no doubt that there is grace in the sacraments of the Church, and that God uses the sacraments of Baptism, Confirmation, Confession, Communion, Marriage, Ordination and Extreme

Unction as channels of grace to the souls of those to whom these sacraments are given. Yet this is really a part of the establishment and maintenance of a relationship with God, expressed and effective through the sacraments.

That relationship is also expressed in prayer. I do not suppose that petitionary prayer for worldly objects is particularly often granted, but non-Christians often confuse the prayer which asks for things with the prayer that asks for grace. Prayer for a better mind, for a remission of sins or a capacity for love is, I believe, always granted in some degree. A prayer to be brought closer to God, to be freed from some of the encrustations of self which come between man and God, is never wholly rejected, and if often enough repeated and urged with sufficient real desire changes the soul.

The soul is also changed by human relationships. Everyone who loves us, everyone who is even fond of us, does us good and the more good in proportion to the unselfishness of their love. Everyone we love, or are even fond of, shapes our souls towards heaven, if our love is a genuine and unselfish reaching out and not merely a reflection of self-love at its most extreme. The most trifling act of service that we perform out of love for others develops the power to love that is in our souls. These things are true where there is no religious belief; there are good non-religious people and their goodness grows out of their love for others.

The Christian psychology is however alone—or shares the merit only with the highest reach of other religions—in being an effective and dynamic psychology, because it brings the love of God to reinforce the love of man. The core and centre of human unhappiness, of the unhappiness that can last a lifetime, is self-regard. No person who truly thinks of others and not of himself remains permanently and wholly unhappy, though he may experience great griefs. Nobody who thinks always of himself can be anything but unhappy, since he must always be disappointed, and resentful of a world which does not concentrate its attention on him.

The Christian psychology, full of grace, developed in prayer, aiming at the love of God and man, is the strongest psychology which can develop the soul towards peace.

It achieves its effect by the grace of God, but also by substituting a truth for an untruth. The untruth is that self-regard, if only successful, will make a man happy. That untruth is contradicted by all experience of life—selfish and conceited men are seldom happy, but are notoriously inadequate and sad. The truth is that unselfishness and love for others give a peace and happiness which only come when they are not sought. That again, disregarding the question of Christian belief, is confirmed by all personal experience. Who are the happiest people, with fewest cares? They are the least selfish.

Again one may ask, is it likely that the religion which is based on this unexpected truth about human nature it itself an untruth? Would an untrue religion be likely to come telling us the greatest truth about ourselves?

5

Now let us suppose some great Professor in Atheism to suggest to some of these; that all is a mere dream and imposture; that there is no such excellent Being, as they suppose, that created and preserves them; that all about them is dark senseless matter, driven on by the blind impulses of fatality and fortune; that men first sprang up, like mushrooms, out of the mud and slime of the earth; and that all their thoughts, and the whole of what they call Soul, are only various action and repercussion of small particles of matter, kept awhile a moving by some mechanism and clock-work, which finally ceases and perishes by death. If it be true then (as we daily find it is) that they listen with complacency to these horrid suggestions; if they let go their hope of everlasting life with willingness and joy; if they entertain the thoughts of final perdition with exultation and triumph; ought they not to be esteemed most notorious *fools*, even destitute of common sense, and abandoned to a callousness and numbness of Soul?

Richard Bentley. *The Folly of Atheism. A Sermon.* (1692)

WE ARE nowadays less ironical about atheism than Richard Bentley, the great Master of Trinity College, Cambridge, who gave no quarter to what he conceived to be error, in theology, in classical scholarship or in his own College. Yet by the end of the seventeenth century, within a few years of the first publication of Newton's Principia, he had already identified the basic arguments of scientific atheism in almost the form in which they are still advanced today.

The essential argument of atheism is that God does not exist, the Soul does not exist, the spiritual world does not exist, because everything can be explained in material and scientific terms, including the nature and existence of man, his mind, and at large the whole universe. We are presented with a natural scientific explanation, and that explanation has been expanded and classified by the great increase in knowledge since the early days of science in the seventeenth century.

Science has indeed removed the need for some of the spiritual hypotheses that have at time been put forward. We do not need to introduce God to explain rational thought; the computer shows that. We do not need to introduce God in order to explain the development of man; Darwinism is plainly true in its essentials. We do not need to introduce God to explain life; it is probable that life began from the accidental association of inorganic chemicals early in the history of the world. In short all the theories which give direct spiritual explanations for normal natural events, such as angels pushing the stars round the heavens, are redundant.

This does not remove the possibility of God; it merely removes the necessity to invoke God in order to explain particular phenomena. These are not in fact the phenomena on which the greatest stress has ever been laid in the traditional arguments for the existence of God. Knocking away these arguments does not for instance destroy the basic argument of St. Thomas Aquinas. St. Thomas based his argument on the idea of God as a first cause in nature, not as a series of little local causes, and science can no more show a first cause now than it could in the middle ages. But there can be no doubt that the removal of these particular cause arguments has shaken public faith.

Nor is this surprising. Miracles have always played a large part in converting people to religion, and particularly in the conversion of the mass of people, who are, very reasonably, more impressed by signs and visible proofs, than by conceptual arguments. The apparent modern miracles, like the release of energy in nuclear bombs, have been on the side of a science whose popular interpretation has normally been materialist.

This has had its effect. The modern age is one in which it is harder for the ordinary man to take a religious view of his life. A materialist science may not, and in my view does not, answer the most important questions that can be put to it, but it has revolutionized the world in which men live. Whereas mediaeval man actually saw a magical God as the king of an inexplicable world, modern man can see God as a piece of magical lumber, not needed in a world that science has fully explained, and it has explained many of the problems of his own immediate environment, which must impress him.

This tendency to materialism has been strengthened by the impersonal quality of modern social life, its vast scale of organization, its lack of stable relationships. Religion, and particularly the Christian religion, is a matter of relationships, and of quite simple relationships, with God and our neighbours. It is nourished by good relationships such as the relationships of a village or a monastic community. If starved of relationships, as in a great modern city, the Christian life itself will be weakened. It is not only the Church of England which has found that religion has a natural quality in a country village which it loses in the lonely tower blocks of a great city.

In considering this modern materialism we must however put its own doctrine to the question. Atheism tends to argue that religion is not true, as though it followed from this that atheism were true. What we have to do is to examine the relative likelihood of two hypotheses, to see which is the more probable. We cannot merely assume materialism to be true because we find religion difficult to believe. We can of course reject both and leave ourselves without an explanation.

What is the essential difference between religion and scientific atheism? Surely it is this. Religion supposes that the great reality of the world is spiritual, by which is meant that there is an energy and consciousness, present in God but also present in man, which is not open to material observation, and is not limited by time. Scientific atheism supposes the opposite, that everything that is real is either capable of material observation, or theoretically capable of material observation (science does not hold that physical objects do not exist because they are too remote or too small to be observed). It supposes also that everything is limited by time, and operates in time; it has to suppose this because the logic of science is dependent on cause and effect, and cause and effect are purely temporal concepts. If I catch cold today and die tomorrow that is demonstrative of scientific causation; if I catch cold today and die yesterday that is the overthrow of science.

We have therefore to consider two systems, either of which might explain the world as it is, and both of which pretend to do so. One says that the real energy of the world, the energy which originally created it and is still, and alone, capable of redeeming it, is a spiritual energy, not normally capable of being materially observed and operating outside the limits of time. The other says that the world and universe is all there is or can be, that everything in it is material, and potentially capable of observation, and that everything in it follows the course of time, with the footfall of days following each other and the past irrecoverable.

One thing is immediately apparent. Once the two hypothesis are put side by side it can be seen that the alternative needs to be argued. In the middle ages religion may have benefited from the case for science not being understood. In this century it is the case for science which has been too generally assumed. We have already gone a long way when we recognize that the argument for science is by no means obviously right; that it cannot just be assumed to be right without further inspection.

On inspection the case for atheist scientism has certain weaknesses. The first is its dependence on time. This makes is vulnerable. A single instance of a prophecy fulfilled, other than by coincidence, a single premonitory dream, like Abraham Lincoln's dream of his own lying-in-state, accepted as a genuine premonition, and the absolute rule of time is destroyed. At once we move from a regular world, open in principle to human inspection, to a mysterious world in which the most fundamental laws of science do not invariably apply.

It is the same with miracles. Admit a single miracle—other than healings merely dependent on suggestion—admit a single genuinely miraculous miracle, and the laws of nature are suspended. But by what? The laws of nature cannot be suspended by themselves, but must be subject, once a miracle is accepted, to intervention from outside nature.

This is well understood by scientists of the materialist school. That is why they cannot approach paranormal events, even of the most trivial kind, except in a spirit of downright hostility, quite alien to the open-minded attitude with which they are accustomed to approach ordinary phenomena. A theory which is destroyed by a single contrary instance—a balloon which can be pricked by a single pin—is indeed in a perpetual state of strain, and every alleged instance of the paranormal, however trivial, has to be shown to be fraudulent or explained away.

Obviously a Christian, given all the major and minor miracles of the Old and New Testaments and in the history of the church, feels that there is ample evidence that, as Hamlet said, 'there are more things in heaven and earth, Horatio, than are dreamed of in your philosophy'—a quotation that has only become a cliché because people believe that it represents a truth. Apart from the Christian religion, apart even from the miraculous claims of other religions, there is the evidence of modern research.

Admittedly experiments in telepathy, precognition and so on are hard to repeat and are not all free from suspicion of trickery or ill faith. But it is hard to believe that all the results which cannot be squared with the ordinary operation of the laws of probability are false. These experiments have for me little positive interest; they do not show any new value in the world; but they have great negative significance, for they are hard to square with the materialist hypothesis.

In materialism there must be no prophesy, no miracles, no paranormal phenomena. Those who prefer the materialist alternative have to set themselves that rule and stay inside it, for once admit any of these things, on even one occasion, and you admit something outside material science, and destroy the unity of the system.

To reject all miracles may appear to be an act of common sense; in fact it requires one to defy a great deal of evidence. Many miraculous events are better attested than the normal run of historical events of their period.

That however, while it makes the system vulnerable, and puts it as it were continually on the defensive, is not its real weakness. Scientific materialism is an assertion of a proposition that becomes more and more unbelievable as one considers it. It maintains that the real character of the universe is what the most intellectually evolved animal on a middling planet of a minor star is able to perceive, using his power of reason and his five senses, and supported by instruments of observation which by use of reason he has been able to make.

It does not maintain that this is just part of the reality, but that it is either the whole of it, or so unavoidably all that he can appreciate that it is idle to enquire in any other way. It first reduces man to a purely animal evolutionary character, framed by the automatic operation of general laws, and then endows him with so great a capacity as an observer, that anything he is not capable of observing is excluded from reality.

We know certain things which make it likely that this is false. We know that there are many recently discovered phenomena which man is incapable of sensing without instruments, including most kinds of wave, except for light and sound.

To start with therefore, this supreme observer is known to be defective, or very limited, in the senses he possesses with which to observe. Some of these deficiencies can be made good, perhaps only partially, by instruments: we cannot really understand what the universe would look like to a being which would not see light waves, but could 'see' X-rays. There are no doubt still physical phenomena which have simply not been discovered, in the way that X-rays used not to be known, and of course the scientific hypothesis can contain 'miracles' which are merely natural events whose causes are not yet understood.

We know also that the human observer is badly placed to understand the universe. His life, and even the life of his species, is extremely short relative to the events of the universe. He is not at the centre of the universe, nor is he able to see the whole of it, even with the help of his most powerful instruments. Nor, looking at the smallest things, do his finest instruments enable him to see the way in which its smallest parts operate.

For man to assert that there is no God because he cannot see him—though if he attends he can in some sense know God—is somewhat like an ant in Arizona asserting that there is no such being as the President of the United States because he has no sense data which prove to him the President's existence. The ant might have the better of the argument in the anthill, but he would still be wrong.

Scientific materialism fails then on two grounds. It puts forward the observations of a partial, and inadequate, observer as though they were general and absolute; it requires a belief in the impossibility of miracles which is far harder to accept than the belief that miracles are possible, however cautious one may be about accepting the miraculous character of any particular occurrence.

The greatest scientists, and this is true particularly of Newton and Einstein, have adopted a quite different attitude. Both were humble before the universe. Neither believed that science in its present stage had done more than begin the process of discovery. Neither believed that there were scientific laws which excluded the possibility of further discovery about the real nature of the universe. Both believed that the universe had a harmony which could be regarded as religious in character.

Let me then put together the materialist and the religious view. At the end of the materialist view we come to an area of mystery; some of that mystery will eventually be cleared up by the continuing process of scientific discovery. But the mystery is not a small proportion of unknown territory which will shortly be mapped and settled. It is almost everything, and what we know, even now, is almost nothing.

In this area of mystery, which is still so large, still the whole of the sky with perhaps one star of scientific knowledge shining in it, man has had from the beginning another type of guide and another type of knowledge. When he was even more ignorant than he is now, he had a religious message that the mystery of the universe was rational and not irrational, was benign and not hostile, was harmonious. This at first, in primitive and heathen religions, fixed itself to particular places and took magical and multiple forms.

As human history developed so did religion, both through early priests and philosophers, then with the great advance of Judaism and with the great new revelation of Jesus, coming as he did not to destroy the Jewish law but to fulfil it. Unlike the microscope and the telescope, religion does not replace mystery with apparently clear-cut and precise patterns of fact. So long as we are alive, it is a light shining in the darkness, though we may believe that in the next world it will be broad day.

The question we have to consider is whether we should accept the limitations of scientific materialism, with its inherent arrogance, or whether with Newton and Einstein we should look out at the mystery beyond as something vaster and more significant than the limited and partial reality which is all that science can show.

If we accept that the mystery is the reality, and not the little invasion science has made into mystery's vast territories, then we have to consider further whether religion, not a particular religion, but the common substance of all religion, should be accepted as the best guide to this great mystery. And if we accept the validity of religion, we have to consider which religion we can best rely on. It is at least not irrational to decide these questions for religion generally, and in particular for Christianity, and against materialism.

I do not pretend for a moment that this line of argument is sufficient to confute scientific materialism. It is not intended to achieve so big an aim in so small a space. All I want to do is to show that there are arguments on which a reasonable man can come down on the religious side, not simply because he thought it the more desirable, but because it seemed to him the more reasonable.

These are in fact the arguments which have convinced me. I am confirmed in accepting them by the development of modern science, as I understand it. At one time science made for simplicity. Broad principles, like the principle of evolution, made very complicated natural processes seem quite straightforward. The atomic theory, when atoms were still thought of as nice, chunky solid little objects, like billiard balls, made the structure of nature seem simple and readily accessible to the human mind.

This move to simplification proved to be a temporary phase. As science progressed it came into contact with more and more complex structures, less and less solid, and less and less easy for the human mind to grasp. What had seemed first in poor focus, then in sharp focus, swung out of clear focus again. Science does not therefore offer a simple realistic alternative. The reality of the rock in the road is no longer that of a solid rock, but of a pattern of molecules made up of atoms which are themselves like the universe largely empty, but have particles of energy moving inside them. The scientist's rock is as hard to visualize as Bishop Berkeley's idealist rock, and kicking it will neither confute nor confirm one or the other.

45

The science which has influenced the twentieth century, and still greatly influences most people and only too many scientists, is however this simple and primitive science which can develop television sets and build bombs and cure diseases and send men to the moon. This is the science of the scientific miracle, and if it is not examined closely it can be taken to be the explanation of all things.

When science was first disturbing the roots of faith, it was the intellectuals who saw the force of the scientific argument. It was people accustomed to abstract thought who were the first to lose their faith in religion, while ordinary people still saw religion as the natural explanation of the universe. They were not all very religious, but religion was the basis of their understanding of the universe.

Now I think it is the other way on. Science is ceasing to be a threat to the religion of men accustomed to abstract thought. The development of science itself has gone beyond that stage; it can be seen that the argument for simple scientific materialism is either very weak or at most inconclusive. Yet ordinary people now accept the preeminence of science, and even if they conform to religious observance, often have an uneasy and out of date fear that science has disproved religion.

They should put to themselves these propositions.

1. Materialist science believes that all things are moved and made of energy, and that this motion of energy is all that is real in the universe.

2. Idealist religion believes that the physical world is moved by energy, but that there is a spiritual world, on which the physical world depends, which is made and moved by love.

Which, they should then ask themselves, corresponds more closely to their own experience?

6

ASIDE FROM asking whether religion is true, we should ask whether religion works. It is certainly possible for a theory to work which is not true, and common for a theory to work which is only partly true, but if religion does not work it can have no meaning. If religion did not work on the lives of men, then it could be true but would not matter. Nobody need bother about an elevated being in the sky who has nothing to say to us. If that were all that God amounted to, there would be no practical difference between belief and non-belief; we might all just as well be atheists in respect of a God who did not concern himself with men.

If religion works then the evidence of its effect can only be found in human life, in the lives of individuals and in the lives of human societies. Are God-loving people different from those who have no care for God? Are they in some way better? Are societies which respect God different from societies which reject God? Are they better than societies without faith, or with altars loaded with sacrifices to anti-God?

It is this evidence which should be looked for, first of all. Does God make a difference? Is it a difference for the better?

Perhaps the first question is the easier to answer, because it is so very obvious that God does make a difference. Wherever one looks for the evidence of that, it is to be found. The lives of people of strong religious belief are different from the lives of those with none, or with little belief. Their aims are not the same, their standards are not the same, their attitudes towards themselves and other people are not the same. There is no similarity, the two cases are completely different. Nor is this merely a question of genius. We can no more compare ourselves to St. Francis than to Shakespeare; we do not expect to be given religious genius any more than we expect to be given literary genius. But we can compare ourselves to ordinary praying believers who have fully turned their spirits towards God; we can see that they are different from us.

The same is true of successful religious societies. I doubt if there has ever been a fully religious nation, except perhaps for a short time, but there are societies of prayer and contemplation. They are different from other societies. A monastery is different from a lay college; it is different in motive, in principle, in atmosphere, in effect.

This difference is even clear enough when religion is mixed with other and perhaps corrupt material. An army fighting a religious war may be committing a blasphemy, if religion is being mixed with the ordinary motives of nationhood and the search for power. Yet a religious war is like no other war; it engages elements of human nature which are not involved in the lesser motives of patriotism or aggression. Such wars are different, and the leaders of such wars, men like Mahomet or Cromwell, make different claims on their followers.

The second question is whether the difference involved in religion is a difference for the better. Not always so; the history of every religion includes a history of crimes not only committed in the name of religion, which is at worst a matter of hypocrisy, but actually because of religion. I killed, I burnt, I tortured in God's name; that is the terrible claim of the inquisitor, and there is no religion wholly free of it. Nor should it be excused, though it should be understood.

Religion simultaneously engages man's deepest emotions and presents him with his highest good. There is no emotion as profound as the religious emotion; it has all the power of man's relationship with what is outside himself and with what is inside as well, it is his relationship with the cause of the universe and the cause of his own being. It is, as a fact, stronger than the fear of death; the martyrs of every religion go to their death singing. It is stronger than the love of men and women for each other; it is stronger than the ties of family. It is the human force to which no other force is equal.

Nor is there any object equal to the object of religion. Whether it be true or false, the idea of the Godhead is the sum of all ideas. It is the host held up by the priest; it is the sun in the sky; it is love and it is sacrifice; it is humility and it is power; it is the energy of the universe; it is the peace of

48

a summer evening in England; it is not only truth but the perfect pattern and fountain of truth; it is not only beauty but the true origin and source of all beauty; it is the star-scattered darkness of the sky at night, condensed into the space of a needle's point; it is the mother to the baby or the father to the child; but again it is love, human, personal, faithful and without limit.

Such an object, sought with such passion, cannot fail to heighten all the energies; if those energies are, by some defect, associated with evil means, then that very thing which is the source of all human good gives an unlimited force to the evil which becomes associated with it. It is the master energy of a human personality, and may drive evil as well as good in that personality to its extreme limit.

Yet no one can say that this is the normal case. The normal case is itself very imperfect. It is no doubt your case, as it is mine. In the normal case the idea of God is present imperfectly in the mind, not only imperfectly but occasionally as well. We see in a glass darkly, or like a schoolboy looking in a darkened mirror at an eclipse of the sun, with two or more layers of withdrawal between ourselves and the idea. We look in that mirror only from time to time, and see only shadows there. The idea of God is not always with us; the notions of the world are with us much more often. Yet even one half glance, through a stage of many darkened mirrors, and years ago, can sweeten a life and at the last can save a soul. Once there has been that glimpse, hope is never lost.

We are not, most of us, good people. We do not live our lives as though God existed, or as we would do if we had any full consciousness of that fact. We certainly do not lead our lives as though God had died for us, or as we would surely do if we had any full consciousness of that still more extraordinary fact. Yet we do not lead our lives wholly as though God did not exist either. Judged by the standards of perfection we are nothing; yet there is some glint of hope, some touch of love, which makes us, if God wills it, indigestible to the other side.

Who can doubt that these glimpses of the idea of God, particularly if they are reinforced by steady if unilluminated prayer and, one of the greatest fortunes of human life, by the practice of regular and tranquil attendance at Church, tend to make ordinary inadequate sinful people a little better, and certainly a great deal less bad than they might otherwise be. Men remain proud, greedy, selfish, and whatever else their sins are, but not totalitarian in their sins, not without limit, not without the grace occasionally to do better.

So it is with most of us. We can honestly believe that religion works to make us better, even though religion does not succeed in making us very good. Yet apart from those whom religion reinforces in some lonely error, or makes proud or cruel, and apart from that vast majority whom religion helps but leaves in mid-ocean to battle on through storms of their own selfishness, there are those whom religion in some fuller way sanctifies.

Roman Catholics like myself, in the days when writing about religion was polemical, were accused of worshipping the saints, or at least allowing them undue importance. But the saints are the proof of religion. If God did not sanctify the human soul, what would he mean to us? He might be a very good God for Martians or for geese, if he sanctified them, but if he did not sanctify human beings, he would have no meaning for us. He would be no better than the God of the eighteenth-century Deists who wound up the world like a clock, and then left it to its own devices, presumably spending the rest of eternity playing billiards.

It is the spirit of God shown for us in the sanctification of the human spirit that shows us what God is, supremely so in Jesus, truly so in all his saints.

Saints are, when all is said, against nature. It is natural to be selfish, for selfishness is part of the equipment of self-preservation which has preserved the human species; it is indeed natural to love, but not to love wholly without self regard. The sweetness of the soul that lives with God and in whom God lives is above nature, and the actions of those souls that have been brought to this level cut across the natural urge to lead the life of self interest which all the rest of us in fact lead.

The rest of us are in prayer sometimes or occasionally, the saints always. We love God faintly when we remember, the saints wholly and all the time. We put ourselves first and others or God second. The saints put themselves last, God first and their neighbour second only to God. We love the lovable, the saints the unlovable. We visit the sick, hastily between other appointments; prisoners if a particular friend falls on hard times. The saint makes his ordinary life of works of neighbourly love.

Of course saints are not good all the time; human nature backslides, sanctification on this earth is limited and is never complete. But the contrast is there. In our lives the front door to the soul is ajar and the sunlight of God sometimes lights up the front hall for an hour or two; in the lives and souls of the saints, the whole house is open to the sun, and is bathed in the sunlight of God all the time.

The character of the fully sanctified man, the personality in which love of God and man has become the permanent motive force, is not admired only by Christians or only by religious people. Such a character is admired by those who have no religion at all, or are opposed to religion. They may argue, and with justice, that religion does not often produce such sanctification, that the average of religious people show little sign of this sweetness of sanctity. Yet they do not deny that such a character, when it does appear, is the highest form in which the human character appears, that Mother Theresa, to take extreme examples, is more to be admired than Alexander the Great, or even than Isaac Newton. It is not only a proof of the truth of religion that the belief in God can produce such characters, it is a proof of its power.

The power of religion can also be seen in the lives and characters of nations. The life of nations without a central animating belief is a decay. Indeed nations form themselves around thoughts or ideas, which have their own life-cycle. These ideas are essentially religious in character, though they are not always religious in expression. A nation which has no such idea, or has lost confidence in its idea, is empty inside; like a hollow tree it can continue to stand, and can even put out fresh leaves in spring, but it will not stand the storm.

Different ideas have a different term of life. The stronger the religious idea is—the nearer it is to religious truth—the longer its life. The great religions last at least for thousands of years; nations are formed and reformed around them. Purely philosophical ideas, the religions which exclude metaphysical belief, do not have this lasting power; Confucianism, a sort

51

of philosophical religion is ancient, but Marxist Leninism shows a rate of change and decline which is far more rapid than that of the major religions.

Nevertheless we are experiencing in the West a major crisis of faith. In the non-Communist countries of the European tradition, Christian faith has become a minority belief. The churches are empty, not everywhere but in most places. Some of the churches that are full have congregations with empty hearts.

If religion is the psychological core of the nation, then one should expect this visible decline in faith to cause a decline in the self-confidence and social cohesion of the nations affected. Certainly the religious decline exists; no one questions that. It is seldom doubted that the decline in national confidence exists. But has the one caused the other?

It is not easy to prove the relationship of cause and effect. Indeed one could do worse than to ask one's reader whether his own experience suggests that the decline of religious faith has produced this national decline or not. I would use the argument not of strict proof, but of congruity.

A hundred years ago in England the new, though not the first, assaults of doubt had penetrated the intellectuals, always the most exposed to new ideas, bad or good. Yet the mass of the public, whether observant or not, lived in a strongly religious culture, exposed at every turn to religious ideas and to the affirmation of a morality of absolute right and wrong, based on religious doctrine. The nation did not live a fully or wholly religious life, of course not. But all the citizens of the nation were exposed, continuously and unavoidably, to its religious character. Religion penetrated the soil of Victorian England like rain beating on the ground.

This religion was mixed with national pride, and with the mixed sense of responsibility and greed which constituted the vocation of empire. It was possible to rely on the English people, on the whole British people, as it has been hard to rely on the whole of any other people at any other time. The nation was a self-disciplining body because of shared beliefs, and the basis of these beliefs was religious.

There was a vigour, one could say a puritanism, about these beliefs. Women were expected to be chaste and loyal, and the great majority of them were so; men were expected to be honest and hardworking, and if necessary courageous; the great majority of them seem to have been so as well. The loose woman and the ne'er do well man were despised, probably in all levels of society.

Authority was accepted; the authority of a ruling class and a preaching clergy; the authority of the Queen and the constitution; the authority of the employer and those he appointed as managers or foremen; the authority of teachers; the authority of the law.

This authority became exaggerated and oppressive, particularly perhaps in the case of the authority of the father in his family. But it gave Britain a strength which every nation in the world respected; the British Common Law was taken to be the best law in the world; the British currency made sterling a synonym for trustworthiness; the British businessman did not cheat; the British taxpayer paid his taxes; the thin red line of British soldiers did not run away; to be a British citizen became the proud boast of all Britons, a status in itself envied by the rest of the world.

This discipline was founded more in the fear than in the love of God, but it was the discipline of a people who believed that they lived in God's presence, in hope of his rewards and in fear of his punishments. The discipline shaped their characters, just as much as the indisciplined modern culture shapes ours. It is wrong to think that the Victorians hated being Victorians, or that they would have preferred pot and kaftans and the gay liberation front. They felt liberated because they were masters of their own conduct. The Victorian relied on his own will-power to support him in a way that few people now do.

With this discipline they moved the world. They had chosen the discipline for themselves, in so far as one's own historical culture leaves one choice. They were free men and they recognized that integrity and self-discipline were the conditions of freedom. In their century Britain took the lead industrially, scientifically, in the development of new inventions, in the spread of order and in the spread of freedom. They had a civilizing and a Christianizing mission. Of course they sometimes abused their power, as men do abuse power, but they made possible the self-development of the nations they came to dominate. They made mistakes, but this process of world development was necessary, and no other nation could have been relied upon to do it as well.

I am not putting forward Victorian Britain as a fully sanctified nation; one can see the evil also in Victorianism. I doubt whether there is such a thing, or ever has been such a thing, as a fully sanctified nation. Victorian Britain had mixed religious and material motives; the religious motives gave energy and strength to the material, but the material in some measure corrupted the religious. Yet the Victorian age can be compared to one of those spirits who have had some inklings of religion, who have been aware of religion, but not enough. Religion did raise a whole nation, and has raised other nations, to the role of a fallible but in some measure converted character.

We are not like that now.

7

It is hard to form a fair view of one's own age. Many people in many ages have believed that they lived in a uniquely wicked and decadent time. The brutality of human nature, that primitive creature that always threatens civilization, seems less alarming when looked at from the perspective of history. It is unlikely that we are uniquely wicked, though of course we do have unprecedented powers of destruction.

Nevertheless we have to make some judgement of our own period if we are to understand it. It is a hollow period, hollow in the way that an individual personality can be hollow if there is no vital motive. The emptiness is particularly obvious in the advanced industrial countries of the west; it is also observable in the cynicism of the leading groups of Communist society, though China may still be relatively free of it.

Britain certainly now suffers from this depression of lack of purpose, of lack of faith. In the individual such a depression often comes in middle age; achievements which were greatly valued no longer satisfy, work which used to be a pleasure becomes a burden. The flow of ideas dries up.

Britain has, it is true, been in decline as an international power for at least the whole of this century. Yet it is the will to act which has been most seriously eroded, a far more serious loss than the loss of possessions or of power.

The energy of a man depends on the life of the idea that is in him; the energy of the nation depends on the life of the idea that is in the nation. This is the true libido, the psychological force which moves the human and the social frame. Britain, as she now is, has no such idea. Without empire, without a European purpose, without industrial pride, without God, Britain has become a depressed middle aged power, past the peak of her performance, without the will or energy of her youth.

This is essentially a religious problem, because nothing can offer as valid a motive for action as religion. It is fun to be rich or wise or powerful or fruitful. Yet none of us is destined to be as rich or wise or powerful or fruitful as Solomon, and his conclusion on the matter is definite:

'I . . . was king over Israel in Jerusalem. And I gave my heart to seek and search out by wisdom concerning all things that are done under heaven; this sore travail hath God given to the sons of man to be exercised therewith. I have seen all the works that are done under the sun; and behold all is vanity and vexation of spirit. That which is crooked cannot be made straight; and that which is wanting cannot be numbered. I communed with mine own heart, saying, Lo, I am come to great estate and have gotten more wisdom than all they that have been before me in Jerusalem; yea, my heart had great experience of wisdom and knowledge. And I gave my heart to know wisdom, and to know madness and folly; I perceived that this also is vexation of spirit. For in much wisdom is much grief; and he that increaseth knowledge, increaseth sorrow.'

If there were no religious answer to be found, then the life of man, or the life of the nation, would have no point. It would be movement in a vacuum: it would be a story told in words which have no meaning. A nation without religion, or an individual without religion, is a lost being, constantly seeking what can never be found, a mortal objective of lasting significance. Yet Britain and Western Europe have lost their faith; the institutions of faith are still there, some of the moral and social habits of faith are still there, but faith itself has gone. The whole of European civilization is near to becoming like one of the church museums of the Soviet Union, in which the edifice of faith is shown to tourists by the uniformed guides of systematic unbelief.

This loss of faith extends into every aspect of a nation's life. Loss of faith erodes respect for all the national institutions. In Britain we inherit, and still possess, the advantage of a national respect for law; we honour our law. That honour is in decline; not only is there a steady increase in almost every form of notified crime, but, to common knowledge, those who are not criminals are less scrupulous about complying with the law. Not paying taxes, petty smuggling, car offences, drug offences, the crimes of the non-criminal classes, have become much more common and much more widely accepted.

Loss of faith undermines the family. Family life depends absolutely on the acceptance of responsibility and hard work for the sake of others. Christian family life is at its happiest when the love inside the family reflects and is strengthened by the love of each member of the family for God. Where sexual love is lit by faith it too has a different character. Of course Christians feel the joys as well as the temptations of simple erotic love, and realize the beauty it can have. But it is not enough, when love is absent.

Loss of faith affects all social relationships. In a religious nation all people recognize the equality of being the same spiritual beings, of sharing the same God and the same immortal future. It affects also the creative life of a nation. We now live in a period when all the arts seem to offer the same warning of despair.

With religion there is every kind of hope. All the fears of life, all the disappointments of life, all the agonies of life, depend on temporal mischances. It does not matter to a man if he dies alone in a gutter if he dies close to God; it does not help a man to live in prosperity and success, if he lives far from God. With true religion despair is impossible, for the mercy of God is infinite; without true religion despair is inevitable, for life can be nothing but a series of pointless vexations terminating in death. Hope is therefore intrinsic to religion, and despair is intrinsic to unbelief.

It is despair which we see in the West. We despair in our own civilization because it has been cut off at the root. Ours has been a civilization of endeavour, perhaps to an exaggerated degree; it has been a civilization of personal development, and perhaps it has been too Protestant, too individual. But it has also been the most creative of the civilizations known to us in world history, creative and inspired by ideals of honour and justice.

This despair does not run so deeply in the United States, but then the decline of religion has not gone so far in the United

57

States. It is possible that the confidence which Americans still have in their civilization will help to see us all through. It is a confidence which the rest of us can only admire.

National despair itself has many facets. Some of them are political; the nation responds sluggishly to challenge or to opportunity. Those who stand out, who would be the nation's leaders, are resented and jealously pulled down rather than supported. There can be occasional outbursts of irrational jingoism, like Britain's policy in the Suez crisis of 1956, but there is lack of deep and consistent patriotism. Public opinion seems brittle; at one moment it appears very determined, at the next it cracks. This makes sound policy hard to achieve, and manipulative politicians, who are content to express the instant mood of successive moments, are only too likely to win power. The nation behaves like a nervous and insecure man; it is jealous, depressed and unstable.

Individual citizens, even those who do not fully share the national mood, find that they are forced to take short views. Individual conduct is pressed into the mould of national conduct. The disciplines of national life fail, because they are not properly supported. Inflation tends to be the result of this failure of discipline in economic policy, because politicians are forced, or believe themselves to be forced, to accept short-term national demands.

Sectional demands are strengthened. As there is no national purpose, sectional purposes, which can readily be seen, gain what should be national sympathies. This leads to sectionalism in economic affairs, particularly in trade unions and trade monopolies, and, by the same logic, to sectionalism in provincial and national attitudes. Demands for the break-up of the nation, socially or regionally, begin to be made, and may be impossible to resist. Individuals express their consequential despair by emigration.

Of course any comparison of historical periods is misleading. There are many qualities in which twentieth-century Britain stands to be preferred to the nineteenth century. That may include the pre-eminent virtue of compassion; though are we all that compassionate? But in the sense in which religion is the golden thread of energy in the life of a nation, the twentieth century is lacking in energy; the absence of religion has left Britain with no sense of purpose.

How can one consider reviving the religious belief of a nation? It is more likely to be revived in failure than in triumph. If one listens to the self-glorification which came at the end of Britain's religious period, one can hear the false note of self-praise.

Land of Hope and Glory, Mother of the Free,
How shall we extol thee, who are born of thee?
Wider still and wider shall thy bounds be set;
God who made thee mighty, make thee mightier yet.

That is the prayer to Mammon, addressed to the Christian God. The Christian God is not a God to whom one can properly, or perhaps safely, pray 'wider still and wider, shall thy bounds be set.'

Is it possible that humility could lead to a new recovery of religion in Britain, or in the West? Only if it is a humility expressed in repentance, and if the repentance expressed regret at our failure to carry out God's will and not, as it only too often does, regret at God's failure to carry out our will. Can one be sure what God's will for a nation is? I would think that a nation, like an individual, has to start by learning spiritual truths. The obvious road for a nation is the road of doing, but, as for individuals, it is often a road which leads nowhere. What is needed is the road of being or becoming, the inner transformation which is expressed, however inadequately, in outer action. That is the road for individuals; how can it not be the road for nations?

8

IF ONE feels love for a nation it is not for its wealth or power, but for its character and faith. It is the character of the British, crossgrained and obstinate as it is, that has seen the British through so many crises of history, their strength of character and the twenty miles of sea that has defended them from their enemies. It is the character of America, that blend of realism, hope and Yankee resilience which has made the United States so great a nation, and it is the character rather than the greatness which is attractive.

Yet in both nations the national character was founded on a religious faith which is now in visible decline, and the decline of religion has foreshadowed the decline, particularly in Britain, of the nations. If I have a fear for the future of both nations it is not economic or military or even in the ordinary sense political or social. It is that a nation cannot live without a metaphysical faith, cannot merely live by nationalism and self-interest. A nation in which the sense of religion dies, quickly begins to die herself.

Both Britain and the United States have been formed by the influence of reformed Christianity. That is not to say that they are purely Protestant, in the Calvinist or even the Lutheran sense. The whole Christian tradition, the broad, strong and ancient tradition of the Catholic Church, is in them. But the tradition of reform, the emphasis on the individual conscience, is in them as well. That is not incompatible with strict Roman Catholic orthodoxy; Sir Thomas More, the most English of all the saints, was a martyr for the authority of the Papacy, but was also a martyr for the independence of his own conscience.

It is not, I think, necessary that the faith of a nation should be held universally, nor is it possible. We do not fully know what the ordinary Englishman of the middle ages felt about religion, but certainly many were anti-clerical, and the sense of phrases like hocus pocus, which Tillotson believed to be 'nothing else but a corruption of hoc est corpus, by way of ridiculous imitation of the priests of the Church of Rome', suggests that there were always some sceptical peasants or apprentices. Certainly the stronger faith of the nineteenth century was partial and not all-conquering. Yet the marks of an age of faith are clear enough, and so are the marks of an age of scepticism.

The fortunate people of an age of faith live and work and pray as though always and directly in the presence of God. Such an age will be likely to produce great saints, and may also produce great sinners. Yet even the sinners are likely to share the underlying faith of their community, as will the great majority of ordinary people.

There is in such ages some reversal of the sense of reality. Perhaps I may explain it in terms which may make sense to those who have no such religious feelings: if one looks out to sea and senses the vastness and depth of the ocean, one feels that the ocean is real, and the affairs of the cities of men are tiny and temporary and irrelevant.

That is the order of reality which anyone will also have who feels the immediate sense of the presence of God, for God is much greater than the ocean or the sky at night. For an age of faith reality consists in the matter of the faith; for an age of unbelief, reality consists in the immediate accidents and interests of human life.

There is therefore a tranquillity about an age of faith which underlies the shocks and alterations of its history, just as there is a tranquility in the life of the individual of religious temperament. What happens, good or bad, is of the surface. The reality is of the depths, and the reality is both unchanging and eternal.

This reversal of reality has implications throughout the life of a nation. Let us take, for instance, the attitude towards human suffering. There is one attitude natural to faith: that of compassion, the attitude of the good Samaritan. There is another attitude natural to scepticism: that of sentimentality.

What is the difference between compassion and sentimentality? Compassion is realistic and sentimentality is idealistic;

compassion is other-regarding and sentimentality is self-regarding; compassion is concerned with doing good, sentimentality is concerned with feeling good; compassion involves loving one's neighbour as a reflection of the love of God, sentimentality involves loving oneself because there is no God to love; compassion is founded in truth, sentimentality is founded in falsehood, in the pretence that we have feelings we do not in reality experience.

It is usually true that sentimental people are callous. Indeed it follows from the machinery of sentimentality that they should be so. Sentimentality is an artificial diversion of the instinct of sympathy towards particular and limited objects. Some of the most wicked of the Nazis were very sentimental people, and they lavished this diverted sympathy on plump, pink little Nazi children, who had no great need of it, while leaving skinny little Ann Frank children to their fate.

Both Britain and the United States have become very sentimental countries, countries in which there has been a separation between acts and consequences, both in doing good and in doing evil. This is the age of the long-distance giver and of the long-distance killer, of the man who gives on a tax-deductible basis, and the killer who gives an order to fire a weapon that will maim or kill someone he never sees, someone not even his subordinate will ever see.

In an age of faith the individual must always be a little amused at his own pretensions; this is the sense of humour of the saints, the humour of More on the scaffold. The idea is after all an incongruous one. Here is man, that odd forked radish with a soul, combining the body of a clever monkey with a direct understanding of God. In the light of that incongruity all man's wants and ambitions have an element of the absurd about them. Here is the forked radish dressed in purple and with bay leaves in his hair; he is the Emperor Augustus. Here he is up a ladder with a paintbrush; he is Michaelangelo. Here is the forked radish prowling through the East End with a surgeon's knife and a black bag; he is Jack the Ripper. Here he is on his knees; he is talking to God who made the universe, made man, is all-powerful and all-loving. And moreover he is in a particular sense talking to God as an equal, since he has been made by God in his own image, not that God is just another and larger forked radish, but that man, like God, is an eternal spirit.

In an age of scepticism we must be more serious than that. There is nothing to laugh about in the state of man without God. At best man is a relatively intelligent animal on a life-bearing planet of a minor star, a bleakly mortal individual, of a species doomed to extinction, on a planet that will grow cold, belonging to a star that will fail. If he is good or bad, it is all one. Neither Stalin nor St. Gregory the Great will be remembered when the sun grows cold, in a universe with no reality beyond its physical presence. For the sceptic only the justification of temporary social use can be found for being ethical rather than destructive.

At worst man without a God is a predator among predators, *homo homini lupus*—man a wolf to man. And indeed such has been the experience of the twentieth century. Whatever the crimes committed in the name of God, they are nothing to the twentieth-century crimes committed in the name of Marx, to the crimes of Lenin, or Stalin, or Mao Tse-Tung. Nor are they anything compared to the crimes of the Nazis. The great modern age of unbelief has not been the age of the agnostic, ethical men of benevolence, peering through their pince-nez at the follies of the world, and sometimes compounding those follies with their own. The dominant twentieth-century unbelief has not been the benevolent agnosticism of the Webbs but the murderous atheism of Stalin of whom the Webbs thought so highly.

This murderous seriousness is also a reflection of a mis-placed sense of reality. That is not at all the prerogative of Marxists or secret policemen. In the United States there has been a comparably exaggerated seriousness, almost amounting to worship, in some of the great corporations. The company executive, aiming for a Vice-Presidency as though it were a Cardinal's hat, placing the company first and neglecting his wife and family in order to further the supposed interests of a multinational bureaucracy and to sell more detergent, is a pathetic and almost a lunatic figure. But if you do not know that God exists, how do you know that Procter and Gamble is not God? And if Procter and Gamble might be God, why not the KGB which also offers life and warmth and protection and promotion to its acolytes?

A world without God is more sentimental, more serious, and more cruel than God's world; it is also much more self-centred. Temporarily in the post-revolutionary period of Communist regimes, and still so far as one can tell in China, it has been possible to substitute the state for God and to have men serve the state as their supreme good. Even in Communist states post-revolutionary fervour only lasts for a limited time.

It is one of the central concepts of Christianity that the first duty of man is to love God, and from that flows his second duty of loving his neighbour. In the mind and soul of the saint the love of God becomes so complete in its personation that it is reflected in all the actions that the saint may take. Love God first, and the love of man, difficult as it is, will follow. Equally the absence of God narrows the regard of the soul; the individual sees only himself as an object of concern.

This self-centredness in the absence of religion is not invariable in individuals, but is inevitable in nations; it is part of the explanation of the social deterioration of Western civilization, of which the different types of decline of Britain and the United States are examples. Let us take one instance of the effect of the loss of God, the effect on marriage, the central institution of society.

The sanctified Christian marriage, or the sanctified Jewish marriage, both common enough in the centuries of faith, but somewhat rare now, is one in which the loving presence of God is continually with the family. The Jewish family is one of the most beautiful expressions of love and security in human experience. In such a family the accidents of human life have their place, but it is not the predominant place. The members of the family love each other because they can do no other; they experience the jealousies and pressures of life, they are jealous and angry and selfish like everyone else, but as part of the lower order of reality. The words of the solemnization of matrimony in the Church of England's Book of Common Prayer express what they naturally feel, and not as a hard promise made reluctantly: 'I take thee to my wedded wife, to have and to hold, from this day forward, for better for worse, for richer for poorer, in sickness and in health, to love and to cherish, till death do us part, according to God's holy ordinance, and thereto I plight thee my troth'.

The mortal accidents of poverty and illness are not as unspeakably overwhelming to a married love which reflects a consciousness of eternity. Of course Christians suffer grief and temptation, just as Jesus did, but they know grief and temptation for what they are, as part of what happens, not as the end of all things.

The parents in such a marriage will not be perfect and will probably be very imperfect, but their relationship will have a depth even at moments of strain which will help to support the whole family. As a child who never for a moment doubted his parents' love of each other, I know what that is. Such marriages occasionally fail, but they are entered into with such expectations that at best the commoner causes of failure are to some extent guarded against.

Then contrast this with the real statement so common in the modern Western marriage of unbelief: 'I take thee for my wedded wife because I have found it enjoyable to have sex with you; so long as you continue to be attractive to me and I do not find sex preferable with someone else I expect to continue to be married to you; if you become old or ugly or peevish or poor or ill I shall leave you if you have not already left me; in the meantime I shall cherish you financially and will take you to parties where we can shine before our set.'

To the millions of individuals who suffer from living in such an age of unbelief I must make an apology; I am not mocking their sufferings. I am myself an English Roman Catholic; the divorce rate in England is lower than that of the United States, and Roman Catholics, who form a fair proportion of my friends, are forbidden divorce. Yet of all the weddings I have been to, more than half have already ended in divorce. That is the fact of modern life; the institution of marriage has been so undermined, it has been taken so far from its Christian origins, that it is now more difficult for everyone than it has ever been before.

It is the culture of the time we live in which is at fault; it destroys the basis of the best human relationship, because it has undermined the relationship of man and God.

Yet the decay of marriage carries with it the decay of the future. Of course there are men—Winston Churchill was one—who emerge not greatly damaged from being brought up as children of an unhappy family. Yet we have now reached the point at which the secondary consequences of marriage failure are coming to have an independent life of their own. In particular the children of divorced parents, and increasingly the grandchildren of multiple divorces, often the emotionally crippled children of emotionally crippled children, are in many cases finding social or sexual adjustment virtually impossible for them.

The obvious social and sexual problems, delinquency, drug taking, alcoholism, suicide, promiscuity, inability to keep a job, gambling, violence all seem to be closely related to loss of stability of the home. It is the common experience that they occur in stable and unstable homes, but in a much larger number of cases where the marriages have failed. It is evident that such social problems are on the increase, and the increase has followed the rise in the divorce rate, both in Britain and in the United States.

At the turn of the century in Mamaroneck, just outside New York, there was only one man known to my mother's family who had been divorced; there was virtually no delinquency, apparently no drugs, some alcoholism, suicide was extremely rare, and homosexuality was unheard of though no doubt it existed. We have gained in tolerance, but we have lost in stability. That is certainly not the condition of Mamaroneck today.

It is not, I think, that the loss of religion leads to a loss of morale simply because people cease to obey moral commandments when they are no longer thought to be backed by supernatural authority. No doubt that happens to some extent, and the ten commandments are at least a useful code of discipline. It seems to me rather that the loss of religion destroys two vital parts of the human character; it destroys the sense of proportion and makes temporal advantages, those advantages which Satan offered Jesus during the temptation in the wilderness, seem to be much more important than they are. More importantly, it blocks up the natural fountain of love in the heart, by tempting us all with the sin of Narcissus.

9

In every parish of every Christian community, in every synagogue, there are to be found people for whom the joy of the presence of God is the constant colour to their lives, like the sky behind the trees. For them the ordinary business of life, even worldly business, is carried out as a matter-of-fact part of a life led in God's sight. When one sees a Jew with his head covered, that is a reminder that God is everywhere, and an expression of the belief that one should not appear uncovered before God.

This joy is a part of love, and love is necessary to human society, and particularly to free human society. Without love there is no alternative to coercion if human society is to be held together. The state needs the ordinary attitude of the ordinary citizen to be one of love towards his fellow citizen as well as towards his family.

The unity of nations requires that there should be an integrative force, a force that binds the nation together in a common sense of unity. Religion, and particularly the Christian religion, can provide such an integrative force, just as the integrity of the Jewish people has been preserved by their religion from the time of Moses until the present day.

There are other forces which can help to integrate a nation, including nationalist feeling itself, Marxism and racialism, but religion is the strongest and, as in the case of the Jews, has lasted by far the longest; despite dispersal the Jews are the heirs of an unbroken national tradition which has lasted three thousand years since the reign of King David, leaving aside the period before that.

The way in which a commonly held religious belief integrates a nation is complex. There is first of all the simple fact that the belief is commonly held; people are united in the assertion of the truth of their religion or their church. In the wars of religion, or in the modern quasi-religious war in Northern Ireland, religion becomes the badge of the tribe, and nations define themselves by the doctrines they hold.

That is natural enough; what is less obvious is the need that nations have for non-material values. Man does not live by bread alone. A society which exists only to satisfy the material needs of its members is a society which starves its members spiritually, because they cannot draw ideals or non-material purpose from it. Religion, and religion alone, can redeem man from his sense of isolation.

Society also has a natural tendency towards dissolution, the centrifugal force of anarchy. This was the force against which President Lincoln had to fight in the American civil war, and it is the force which is now threatening to break up the United Kingdom.

Of course one has to consider whether and in what sense we do indeed live in an age of religious decline. In 1729, William Law, one of the greatest of English religious writers, could refer to himself and his readers as living 'in the dregs of time'. St. Augustine's Confessions reflect the similar feeling that prevailed at the time of the decline of the Roman Empire, when the life of Jesus was only about as distant in time as the life of Shakespeare is from our time. It is easy to assume that one of the troughs of the cycle of world history is permanent, and equally easy to assume that the evil in the human nature of one's own period of history is unique, different from the evil of other periods.

What would constitute a serious Christian approach to the problem of our time? It would not be a sort of alternative to Marxism, it would not be a political theory in which a thin skin of Christianity was laid over a materialist political system. Such systems may be good or bad; they have little or nothing to do with Christianity. It would be concerned with faith, with the faith that was taught by Jesus. Of course people who come to hold the Christian faith also come to act differently in the world, and they act differently in proportion to the depth of their faith. But Christianity is not a political doctrine about how people should behave in this world. It is a religious doctrine about the nature of God's relationship to man. Non-religious Christianity soon ceases to be Christian.

Thus in Christianity the base is the invisible world and the superstructure is the visible world; the tree is faith and the fruit is works; the light is in the soul and the action is by the body; prayer comes first and charity follows. Any doctrine of works preceding faith, let alone of Christianity without God, is not only a failure, but a heresy, that is a tempting but false belief which may gravely damage the souls and therefore the lives of those who hold it. Yet equally, as works are the fruit of faith, a faith which tends to no good works is not a full faith, perhaps not faith at all.

The ground of Christianity is Christian belief, and the love of God and man which naturally flows from that belief where it has taken possession of the human heart. It is the belief which has made heroes, those who would for instance not be tempted, who even practised works of charity, in concentration camps; it is also the belief which has made good parents and children, good friends, good workers, good priests. Even with the worst of us when the heart is full of the love of God, some will overflow.

Indeed there are naturally two views of the world. One view, the only truly Christian view, is that the love of God matters and that nothing else matters except as a reflection of the love of God. From that principle flow the most loving human relationships, the fullest sense of beauty, the virtue of compassion, the central virtue of humility. The other is the non-religious view that the only real world is the world of the senses, things that you can touch or see or taste or hear. Who can deny that it is this view of the world which now dominates the actions, arguments, ideals and beliefs of our civilization? And who can doubt that this materialist world view is incompatible with the Christian, is indeed its direct opposite?

In the extreme instance the Christian attitude leads to complete loss of concern for worldly interests, though never, I think, to complete loss of concern for expressions of love or charity in worldly terms. Before her last illness St. Monica, the mother of St. Augustine, had a long conversation with her son about the contrast between worldly and spiritual interests: 'then said my mother: Son, for mine own part I have a delight in nothing in this life, what I should here do any longer, and to what end I am here I know not.'

69

The materialist attitude leads us naturally to the worship of this world's advantages. America is not to be blamed, but is to be pitied, for being the most powerful, advanced country in the world. Christ's Kingdom is not of this world; the Kingdom of Washington is. The American system of capitalism has produced wealth and supported freedom; that is good, but the power of this modernism is so great, that it has become the substitute religion of modern people. The new materialism is now the great anti-religion of the free world, just as Marxism is the great anti-religion of the enslaved world.

I have noted in another book° that the late 1720s in England marked the first point at which men of genius scented the first coming of the modern world, and hated it. Swift's *Gulliver's Travels* (1726) is a general satire on the first appearances of modern life; Pope's *Dunciad* (1728) is the first satire on the abuses of what are now called the media; Gay's *The Beggar's Opera* (1728) is a satire on the corruptions of modern political life; yet perhaps the greatest work of all is Berkeley's *Alciphron* (1732) a dialogue which attacks the freethinkers. Perhaps I may retrace a part of Berkeley's argument.

The debate, set in the form of a Socratic dialogue, is principally between Euphranor, who represents the Christian position, and Alciphron, who represents freethinking. The scene is set in a beautifully written passage†:

'We amused ourselves next day every one to his fancy, till nine of the clock, when word was brought that the tea-table was set in the library, which is a gallery on a ground-floor, with an arched door at one end opening into a walk of limes; where, as soon as we had drank tea, we were tempted by fine weather to take a walk which led us to a small mount of easy ascent, on the top whereof we found a seat under a spreading tree. Here we had a prospect on one hand of a narrow bay or creek of the sea, inclosed on either side by a coast beautified with rocks and woods, and green banks and farmhouses.

At the end of the bay was a small town placed upon the slope of a hill, which from the advantage of its situation made a considerable figure. Several fishing boats and lighters glid-

---

° *The Reigning Error*. Hamish Hamilton, 1974. In the first chapter of this book about the causes of inflation I discussed the causes of the decline of discipline in society including the decline of the discipline of money.

† Alciphron, London, 1732, p. 265 et seq.

ing up and down on a surface as smooth and bright as glass enlivened the prospect. On the other side we looked down on green pastures, flocks and herds, basking beneath in sun-shine, while we in our superior situation enjoy'd the freshness of air and shade. Here we felt that sort of joyful instinct which a rural scene and fine weather inspire; and proposed no small pleasure, in resuming and continuing our conference without interruption till dinner: but we had hardly seated ourselves, and look about us, when we saw a fox run by the foot of our mount into an adjacent thicket . . .'

The full title which Berkeley gave his book is *Alciphron or, the Minute Philosopher. In seven dialogues. Containing an Apology for the Christian Religion against those who are called Free-thinkers.* He explains what he means by minute philosophers*.

'The modern Free-thinkers are the very same with those which Cicero called Minute Philosophers, which name admirably suits them, they being a sort of sect which diminish all the most valuable things, the thoughts, views and hopes of men; all the knowledge, notions and theories of the mind they reduce to sense; humane nature they con-tract and degrade to the narrow, low standard of animal life, and assign us only a small pittance of time instead of immortality.

Alciphron very gravely remarked, that the gentlemen of his sect had done no injury to man, and that if he be a little, shortlived, contemptible, animal, it was not their saying it made him so: and they were no more to blame for whatever defects they discover, than a faithful glass for making the wrinkles which it only shows.

Euphranor. Oh Alciphron! These Minute Philosophers, (since that is their true name) are a sort of pirates who plunder all that come in their way. I consider myself as a man left stript and desolate on a bleak beach.'

This is now the state of the ordinary man. The simplest mediaeval peasant, who had perhaps never travelled ten miles from where he was born, wholly ignorant of any scien-tific understanding of the forces of nature, shared a view of the real character of the universe which satisfied St. Paul,

* Loc. cit., p. 33.

St. Augustine or St. Thomas Aquinas, and would have seemed a wonderful and noble revelation to Socrates, Plato or Cicero. The modern factory worker has available to him an understanding of the physical world which would seem almost miraculous to Newton or Descartes, but his understanding of the spiritual world would seem poverty-stricken not merely to a Christian, but to a pagan of the ancient world. All the thoughts, views and hopes of men have been diminished; it is not the elevated philosopher but whole nations which have been 'left stript and desolate on a bleak beach.'

Nor does one even need to believe Christianity to be true to recognize this. Suppose Christianity were not true and yet still compare it with the commonplace materialist view of the world. Each view would then be inadequate, each would wait upon some further revelation of the real nature of our mysterious universe. But one inadequate view would fill the thoughts, views and hopes of men with love and light and meaning, would nourish men on humility and awe of the divine, while the other would have no meaning, would still be empty, miserable and brief. Those who are Christians are fortunate, but those who are not, to whom faith comes with difficulty or not at all, should be able to see that the Christian explanation is live and near to the truth, and the materialist explanation dead and remote from it.

Indeed we are not talking about things like each other. The Christian explanation is an assertion that the world has a meaning beyond the immediate urgencies of life. The materialist explanation, in all its forms, is an assertion of meaninglessness, or at least that the meaning if it does exist is unknown and probably unknowable. The Christian explanation, because it has meaning, answers to the hunger in human nature for a meaning; the materialist explanation, because it offers no meaning except of the most immediate kind, gives no support to human nature. The materialist explanation might in theory be true, but if it were true we should all be lost souls. And in so far as they believe it to be true, people increasingly behave as though they were lost souls.

At different times the proof of Christianity has been rested on one basis or another. I do not believe that philosophic proofs have, or ever have had, much weight with ordinary men. The ages of faith were based on the experience of faith;

that is to say that people inherited their faith in an atmosphere in which it was natural to keep it, and found in fact that their faith supported them; they experienced the truth in their own souls. For an age of unbelief such a general experience of the validity of faith is not possible. That leaves, as I have already argued, the strongest proof of Christianity, the test Jesus proposed 'by their fruits shall ye know them.'

As Berkeley puts it,* 'I am the readier to undertake this point, because I conceive it to be no difficult one, and that one great mark of the truth of Christianity is, in my mind, its tendency to do good, which seems the North Star to conduct our judgement in moral matters, and in all things of a practic nature; moral or practical truths being ever connected with universal benefit. But to judge rightly of this matter, we shou'd endeavour to act like Lysicles upon another occasion, taking into our view the sum of things, and considering principles as branched forth into consequences to the utmost extent we are able. We are not so much to regard the humour or caprice, or imaginary distresses of a few idle men, whose conceit may be offended, though their conscience cannot be wounded; but fairly to consider the true interest of individuals as well as of humane society. Now the Christian Religion, considered as a fountain of light, and joy, and peace, as a source of faith and hope and charity (and that it is so will be evident to whoever takes his notion of it from the Gospel) must needs be a principle of happiness and virtue. And he who sees not, that the destroying the principles of good actions must destroy good actions, sees nothing: and he who, seeing this, shall yet persist to do it, if he be not wicked, who is?'

There then follows one of the most splendid passages of truth in the English literature of Christianity.

'To me it seems that the man can see neither deep nor far who is not sensible of his own misery, sinfulness and dependence; who doth not perceive, that this present world is not designed or adapted to make rational souls happy; who wou'd not be glad of getting into a better state and who wou'd not be overjoy'd to find, that the road leading thither was the love of God and man, the practising every virtue, the living reasonably while we are here upon earth,

* Loc. cit., p. 274 et seq.

proportioning our esteem to the value of things, and so using this world as not to abuse it? For this is what Christianity requires. It neither injoyns the nastiness of the Cynic, nor the insensibility of the Stoic. Can there be a higher ambition than to overcome the world, or a wiser than to subdue ourselves, or a more comfortable doctrine than the remission of sins, or a more joyful prospect than that of having our base nature renewed and assimilated to the Deity, our being made fellow-citizens with Angels and sons of God? Did ever Pythagoreans, or Platonists, or Stoics, even in idea or in wish, propose to the mind of man purer means, or a nobler end? How great a share of our happiness depends upon hope! How totally is this extinguished by the Minute Philosophy! On the other hand, how is it cherished and raised by the Gospel! Let any man who thinks in earnest but consider these things, and then say which he thinks deserveth best of mankind, he who recommends, or he who runs down Christianity? Which he thinks likelier to lead a happy life, to be a hopeful son, an honest dealer, a worthy patriot, he who sincerely believes the Gospel, or he who believes not one tittle of it? He who aims at being a child of God, or he who is contented to be thought, and to be, one of Epicurus's hogs? And in fact do but scan the characters, and observe the behaviour of the common sort of men on both sides: observe and say which live most agreeably to the dictates of reason? How things shou'd be, the reason is plain: how they are, I appeal to fact.'

As to the effects of Christianity on the individual and on society, this argument is, I believe, irresistible. It is not an absolute proof of the truth of Christianity, but if Christianity be not true, and materialism be true; if St. Paul is wrong and the Minute Philosophers are right; then we are in the situation that the truth makes men miserable and bad, and falsehood makes them joyful and good.

The materialist explanation of life, whether it is the Marxist materialism of the Communist world, or the positivist materialism of the Western world, is indeed death to the individual human spirit, though there are many good men who live in the side alleys of these false cities; if its power were still

74

growing there would be everything to fear, and the end of our civilization would indeed be inevitable and at hand. Yet its power is not growing, even though there may still be great masses of people increasingly exposed to it. Exploiting materialism can be seen, and is seen by many people, to be a violation of man's nature and of the earth on which man lives.

Man's situation is like that of the young heir who comes into the inheritance of a thrifty father. At first he believes that his wealth is unlimited, and that the pleasures his wealth will buy are all that matters in life. After a little while he finds that the bills start to come in, the wealth can be seen to be much less than he thought, and he comes to his pleasures with the depression of familiarity and a jaded palate. Man has been spending the resources of the globe, and trading on his own resources, since science put him in possession of his fortune. He is only now beginning to be conscious of the reckoning, and conscious that the material satisfactions as time goes on satisfy less and cost more. That is not the moment at which one despairs of a man coming to his senses; with any luck it is the moment of repentance.

IO

It was oft my way at assemblies to raise my eyes and regard those present from end to end to see whether in sooth I loved everyone among them, whether my acceptance of the duty to love my fellow men was genuine. With God's help I found indeed that I loved all present.
Joel ben Abraham Shemasiah. *Last Will and Testament* (Early 18th Century)

THE SENSE of the presence of God can arise out of any occasion. It can be inspired by natural beauty, by a beautiful landscape or the sky at night. It can be inspired by man-made beauty, particularly perhaps by music. It can also be inspired by the ordinary events of human relations, and particularly of human companionship.

For the Christian this is particularly evident in the domestic details of the life of Jesus which we find in the Gospels. The last supper, which is the heart of the worship of the Catholic Church, was not a liturgical event; it was a genuine and in some senses an ordinary supper. The bread was much the same as the bread one can still buy from a Jerusalem baker; the wine was no doubt much the same as the wine that is still made on the hills near Jerusalem. When he met the eleven Apostles after The Resurrection, he ate boiled fish and honeycomb.

'Where two or three are gathered together in my name, there am I in the midst of them' does not mean that they must be together in church, or in a formal religious setting. A Christian family can always be said to be gathered in the name of Jesus, and certainly they are never wholly out of the presence of God.

It is strange however that, like all the graces of God, the

76

grace of the sense of his presence, though it can often be re-captured by meditation, comes and goes. It is not only a matter of seeing through a glass darkly, but of seeing through a wavering mist, now so thick that one has to take it on trust that there is anything to see at all, now partly blown aside, but never, on this side of the grave, clearing altogether.

What are the occasions on which one can feel the presence of God most often and most powerfully?

First of all when people are praying together, and particularly when they are praying in a liturgy which takes them back to the historic roots of their religion, and is itself a liturgy of great beauty. As a child I can remember regretting, rather foolishly, the loss to the Roman Catholic Church of the Cathedrals of England. I resented the loss because I felt that these cathedrals had been designed for the Mass, and in particular for the Latin Mass, for Gregorian chant and the great affirmations and prayers:

'Credo in unum deum'
'Agnus dei, qui tollis peccata mundi, miserere nobis'

Now if the Roman Catholic church were still in possession of the great English cathedrals, we should use them to pray in a rather flat vernacular, much less beautiful than the Latin, and much less beautiful than the English of the Book of Common Prayer.

Great cathedrals have their place in prayer; their drawback is that they are so seldom full. Any church which is half empty is a reminder of the congregation that is missing, and simply because they are so large cathedrals are almost always empty. One tends therefore to see cathedrals used to their best only on great occasions, like the recent funeral of Cardinal Heenan or the installation of Archbishop Hume in Westminster Cathedral.

Even then it is rather a different matter. A crowd large enough to fill a Cathedral has to be a very big crowd. It is like going to a football match, one is conscious of enormous numbers of people, of numbers such as one meets only rarely in a lifetime. Such a large body can pray together, but it does not come together quite on a human scale. It is more of a rally than a prayer meeting.

The sense of prayer in a parish church is more moving.

There may be fifty or a hundred people there. They are not there for the show; none of them is an agnostic ambassador present out of duty. They are all there to worship. For the most part they know each other, many as friends, all perhaps by sight. They come as families, and they have seen each other's families grow up, from wriggling and inattentive toddlers, through first communions and confirmation, often to weddings and a new band of wriggling toddlers. They pray for each other in sickness and in death. They do not intrude on each other personally or in prayer, but there is a joint prayer week after week which is a link in a long and strong chain of worship.

Apart from occasions of prayer, ordinary occasions of human friendship can have the same effect. I am not saying that every moment of human sympathy should itself be regarded as having a religious quality, though affection must always tend towards religion. There is a feeling of God's presence in human company in which one is half way to a prayer, and the prayer is at least half way to a blessing.

This sensation is often associated with family life; there is nothing so naturally religious as a family meal; natural religion is associated with friendship and the way in which friends support each other in the ordinary distresses and activities of the world; it is associated with celebration, and the contentment, the good will to all men, that good food, good wine and good company can bring.

These are not ecstatic feelings, nor are they produced by ecstatic occasions; I am speaking of the comfort of one's own hearth, not the ecstasy of romantic love; of the calm and easy love that grows naturally for people one knows well in circumstances of comfort and security.

Religion enters into all the details of life, not as a conscious element of sacrifice, but as a background of love and gratitude. The moment when the husband comes home in the evening, an occasion for tea in England and often for a cocktail in the United States, is one of the cherished moments in most happy marriages. Somewhere there is an unexpressed sense of gratitude to God for the security of that moment. It is the same with the development of children. An all-knowing and all-loving God shares the anxieties of parents—a child is sick and they pray to him—and shares their joys. A God

78

who did not enjoy the happiness of children would be a God worthy neither of respect nor belief. We know from the life of Jesus that he did particularly love children, and in this way the humanity of Jesus shows us the humanity of God.

Human beings are for the most part capable of heroism, but do not all have occasion for heroic lives. For the people of quiet lives it is these thin filaments of the love of God which tie them most securely to God himself. They are not called to be martyrs, and would perhaps only be martyrs by rejecting what is plainly their duty in search of some fancied duty which would have some self-indulgence in it. They might face being martyrs if it came to them, but they will not go to it; rather they will try to avoid it, as did Sir Thomas More, by all possible means. Yet the small gratitudes for the happiness of ordinary circumstances, and the small prayers for the well-being of others, provide an ordinary religious life which can grow in strength like that of the martyr or the saint. We should respect the vocation of ordinary life, for it is the vocation that God gives to the overwhelming majority of souls that he saves.

The connections between these ordinary events and religion are of several kinds. First of all, I think, comes gratitude which can be no less intense for the small than for the great gifts of God. Then there is the connection between a sense of well-being, the physical contentment, say, of a sunny day in spring, and the feeling of harmony with God's creation. Then also there are the thousand duties of everyday life, each of which can be done in the spirit of love.

'Who sweeps a room as for thy laws,
Makes that and the action fine.'

Then there are the numerous relationships of everyday life. It matters very much whether we are polite and friendly to the people we meet, to the bus conductor or the postmen. It matters even more that we should be kind and friendly to those we work with; the executive who bullies his secretary can cause more pain than he would dream of. It matters most of all that we should love and cherish our families, for our families cannot get away from us when they are little, and should not wish to get right away as they grow up.

There is also the inherent sadness of human life, which

79

can only be supported if it is carried together. The happiest lives have tragedy in them and periods of great unhappiness; the most successful lives have failure in them; many lives are neither happy nor successful. Most lives have their times of happiness, but interspersed with times of grief, pain, loneliness and frustration. All these things can best be borne when they are shared, but otherwise can only be borne with difficulty.

There is the weakness of human nature, and particularly of our own nature, and the dependence of that weakness on God; we, who do not even have the patience to endure a toothache or a crying baby, need God's help to lead a life of ordinary regularity, let alone to lead a life of heroic virtue.

There is also the strength of selfishness in human nature. When we most want to turn to other people with love and trust, we find that this rock-like selfishness, which almost all of us have, prevents or limits our affection. To dissolve that selfishness into love and charity for others requires the work of repentance and the grace of God.

This domestic happiness can never be a complete happiness; on either view of man's nature he cannot expect complete happiness in this life. On the materialist view he is a finite being with a mind capable of framing concepts of infinity, a being confined between two nothings before birth and after death. If he considers his situation, which is nothing less than that of impending annihilation, it robs his achievements of all but a trace of their lasting significance. On the religious view he is, in a crude phrase, a square peg in a round hole, an eternal soul in a mortal body, a creature made to know and love God, in a world in which God's presence is never allowed to be complete. Death to him is not the concern it may be to the atheist; it is the way to a better place. But the contrast between his own failures and his immortal duties is infinitely more painful.

The work of ordinary life can bring people to God, and if the work is of value it naturally has a content of love in it. This is most obvious in the case of work, such as nursing or medicine, which is of obvious good to other people (there is a conflict when such work, as with medicine in the United States, becomes so very highly paid that the pay rather than work can become an end in itself). Yet less vocational types of work can also give the same satisfaction. Farmers obviously get satisfaction from growing food; masons and carpenters get satisfaction from providing housing.

Men and women in such jobs often regard their work as the only real work. Given the complexity and specialization of modern life, many more indirectly useful professions have the same claim. A farmer cannot produce food efficiently without the services of agricultural engineers, veterinary surgeons, agricultural chemists, transport workers, and even accountants. It is natural to take a pride in work which is obviously useful, and near the end of the chain of production; it is understandably more satisfying to grow wheat than to make the weedkiller which raises the yield on the wheat crop. Yet making weedkiller is equally a useful function, a work of service to one's neighbours.

In the life of the village or the small town work itself produces constant opportunities for neighbourliness, and for the exercise of Christian virtue merely by doing one's work well and conscientiously. It is possible in such conditions for a man to look round his neighbourhood and examine his conscience about the duty of love—does he love his family? Does he love his customers, those who work for him or those for whom he works? It is possible to build a collective Christian relationship, which is the right relationship for a parish. All of those connections can bring people to God, and God can help people to these satisfying and loving relationships.

The larger the community, the harder it is for people to establish these relationships with each other. It is harder to live a Christian life in the rapid and shallow life of a great city; New York is a city one might go to if one had a vocation to save souls, for it has more than its share of spiritual despair; it is not, except for that purpose, a place of first choice for a man who wanted to save his own soul.

The same is true of the large company. Once one has ceased to be able to know who is taking the decisions that affect one's life, or to know who will carry out the decisions one has to take oneself, one has passed from the direct and personal to the impersonal and even the inhuman. Decisions which are not conceived in human terms are seldom taken with love. That is the worst thing about the great complexity of modern organization and the huge size of modern organization.

II

I HAVE thus come to believe in these propositions: that man is by nature a religious animal; that the ground of all religion is love; that the most highly defined and highest truth in religion is Christian; that human society can never be perfect; that without religion human society must degenerate; that our Western society has so degenerated, in all the countries of the post-Christian culture, in Europe and the lands originally colonized and developed by the European nations overseas.

I do not believe that this decline is inevitable or irreversible. On the contrary it seems to me that the main moving force in the decline of religion is past the zenith of its influence. Religion has declined because man came to worship the modern world and modern science. The triumph of the world always proves false, and man is beginning to see the falsehood of this modern triumph.

In any case if one believes that religion is true one cannot believe that religion will fail. If man is a religious being, he cannot eradicate his religious nature; it can for a time be partly obscured, but the longing for a return to harmony with his true nature will not be resisted for more than a brief period. There is therefore no question of the ultimate failure of religion; there is only the damage to generations left in spiritual poverty by being deprived of the religious understanding which human nature requires.

There is also the question whether our European culture, which was founded on Christianity, can survive without it. Christianity will survive, but will the culture and the values of the culture of Europe, a culture which has proved so creative, and has imposed itself on the whole world? This culture is certainly mortal, and is now fragile; its ghost, like the ghost

82

of the culture of ancient Greece, might linger on, and might help to fertilize the cultures of future nations in future ages, but its loss would be one of the greatest tragedies in human history, and to our generation an overwhelming tragedy.

If this culture is to survive, the religious impulse from which it originally arose not only has to revive—for that will happen—but has to revive in time. What we should pray for is one of those great restorations of religious life which have happened on many occasions in human history, restorations which are indeed one of the principal reasons for believing in the truth of religion.

Can we see what form such a revival might take? In the period since the Second World War there has been a continuing decline in the support for organized religion, a decline which has deprived many millions of people of the comfort and guidance and shared prayer of the churches. That is a loss, and it is particularly a loss for the victims of modern society, such as the disoriented poor and delinquent young in the big cities.

At the same time there has been a revival of interest in the ideas of religion, and a very inadequately prepared revival of interest in mysticism. It is as though we were passing out of one period into another, out of the period in which the emphasis on religion is structural (denominations, canon law, church buildings, liturgy, theology, bishops, parishes) and is increasingly intangible (states of mind, prayer, relationship, love).

Most people, partly because we are all children of our own age, as they become aware of this tendency, approve it. It is natural to contrast the religion of pure spirit, of simple fluent adoration of God, as preferable to the religion of bricks and mortar and collections for the church roof. And of course it is a higher form of religion—our Lord's meeting with Martha and Mary tells us that. It was Martha who served the meal, and Mary who anointed the feet of Jesus.

Nevertheless there is something to be said on the other side. Without the humdrum practical work of institutional religion, pure spiritual religion would not pass from generation to generation. Even a Quaker congregation needs a meeting house. The role of Martha is the more humble role of the two, but both are necessary to each other. In addition, a genuine absorption

83

in the love of God normally makes people happy to join in work on the practical details of religion. A man who is too busy praying to take round the collection plate may be a great saint but is much more likely to be a great humbug.

I certainly feel an unqualified gratitude to the physical historic church. Just as every soldier who died in Britain's wars, including the men who fell at Agincourt, died so that I could enjoy the ancient freedom of the British, so every martyr died so that I could say my prayers. Without the national institution of Britain and the religious institution of the Church, I should not be free and I should have no prayers to say. To those who have given their lives for these institutions—or to these institutions—I am therefore bound eternally to be in debt.

Certainly Jesus himself saw the necessity for both aspects of religion, for bottles as well as for wine. Yet it is natural that the relationship between the two should change. In the Roman Church, the change has tended to coincide with Councils of the Church. The Council of Trent, reinforced—in the way that trends are reinforced when they are coming near their end—by the First Vatican Council, strengthened the Church as an institution. The Second Vatican Council set free the spiritual energy of the Church, if necessary at the expense of the church's institutional order. Pope John, like Noah, let the dove out of the ark.

One can see the historic pattern of development which made the Council of Trent and the creation of the modern institutional church appropriate. It was partly the challenge of Protestantism; it was also the development of the modern nation states of Europe; if the nations were to be organized on a tight central principle, the church had to match that organization. One cannot yet see the historic context of the Second Vatican Council from the same detached point of view. Yet there can be little doubt that it was equally appropriate: the Roman Church is often thought of as slow to move, but in some ways the mood of the Second Vatican Council seems to forecast rather than look back, reminding one more of the world of the decade after it occurred than of the decade before.

The Second Vatican Council was an opening out of the

spirit, characteristic of Pope John himself. It was neither heterodox nor anti-institutional; it was pentecostal in that it bore the signs of the Holy Spirit, but not if pentecostal is taken to imply eccentric enthusiasm or irrational conduct. To the world at large Pope John reasserted the primacy of love in the Christian message, love for all Christians of all denominations, love for those not Christians, reconciliation where reconciliation was possible. This was a repetition of the message of Jesus itself; almost every other interpretation of the life of Jesus is in danger of false emphasis, but the central nature of the doctrine of love is not.

This restoration of the central theme of Christianity coincided with the world's fatigue of organization. The modern world has lifted itself upon organization, the nation state, the national armies, political parties, the communist party, industrial companies, the international corporations, mass trade unions. They allowed man a new control over his environment, but have given him new masters, the bureaucracies of the great organizations themselves.

These great skyscrapers of human organization were and are grouped rather like the skyscrapers of Wall Street, with Trinity Church in the middle. The churches could be seen as another set of organizations, not so large, no longer so powerful, but made of the same stuff, with Bishops instead of Managing Directors and Archbishops instead of General Secretaries.

Yet these organizations themselves were and are coming to be resented, and increasingly so, by those who live in them and under them. Their scale is not human; they cannot be aware of the individual; they cannot care for the individual. They are also, because of their scale, ethically neutral. A decent man who would not oppress for his own sake does not feel himself to have the right to give up on ethical grounds the apparent interest of the corporation he serves. In this respect governments and trade unions are just large corporations.

The church, which was founded under the Roman Empire, one of the most gigantic corporations in the history of man, has from its origins experienced the conflict between its need to protect its own interests and the souls in its charge by corporate counterforce, and the need to avoid the corporate impersonality which can be the death of personal morality. At times it has failed one way—as in the most triumphalist periods of the Papacy—and perhaps more often the other— when the Church was too weak to protect itself or anyone else.

Some of the greatest disputes in religious history—Pope versus Emperor, Pope versus Napoleon, Pope versus the risorgimento, Thomas a Becket versus King Henry II—have sprung from this theme.

Yet whatever may have been true of other periods, the late twentieth century could neither be kept Christian nor reconverted to Christianity by administrative methods. If the Church were simply to be one, and by no means the most imposing, of a number of bureaucracies, then the church would be doomed.

The physical analogy lies with the skeleton and the blood. Without a skeleton, or with a deformed or damaged skeleton, a vertebrate animal cannot operate, cannot stand, run or go down on the knees to pray. Yet a skeleton is only a skeleton, and without the flow of life becomes merely a museum exhibit, dry bones in a glass case. It is the blood which carries life around the body. In the same way the administrative structure is essential to the church; hostility to that structure is as foolish as hostility to one's own vertebrae; yet it is not by itself capable of maintaining the real life of the church; it is the structure inside which the life of the church occurs, but it is not that life, never has been and by its nature never could be.

That life is the love of God; it is worship; it is adoration; it is selflessness; it is repentance; it is love of one's neighbour; it is communion with God. The church is prayer and the fruit of prayer; everything else is subordinate to that, and is valuable as it serves and preserves that, and not valuable if it does not serve or preserve.

Of course this truth is itself capable of perversion and exaggeration. On the one hand it is possible to emotionalize and sentimentalize worship. The value of prayer is not related to the emotional satisfaction of the person praying, which may be high or low in prayer of the most advanced kind. There is always the danger of Pharisaism, of a pseudo-spiritual intoxication which has in it a great deal of pride and self-conceit. One of the great virtues of the Church is the endless experience, the deep wells of dispassionate wisdom, which help to keep a self-serving and self-intoxicating zeal from deluding people.

The life of worship is gradually built up by those very administrative processes which it is so facile to despise. It is true that saints are much more important than Cardinals (though some men have been both) but it is also true that without Cardinals there would be many, many fewer saints. The most selfish and unspiritual of church administrators, the most limited and narrow-minded of Bishops' secretaries, should still be seen as the administrative corps of an army is seen. He is not the man who does the fighting, he does not have that honour, but without him the fighting men would have no arms and no food. And the great majority of church administrators do not deserve even the censure implied by this analogy.

Nevertheless this was not the need of the twentieth century, or was certainly not the chief need. It was not for Martha, but for Mary, that the modern world pined. It was the vial of the spirit that needed to be opened to the world. It is the emptiness of the modern world which needs to be filled.

Our world is one of a confrontation between the false doctrine of Marxism and the meaningless post-Christian materialism of the West. In the third world, as we have the arrogance to call it, the Islamic area and the one Jewish state, though in conflict with each other, are still strongly religious and seem able to throw off some of the temptation of Marxism and the disillusion of the West. It is less certain how far the religions of Asia have the same strength, outside the Islamic area, though Hinduism always determines the character of Indian life.

Yet while we may draw this picture for purposes of description, it would be fatal to rely on it for a motive. If the West were to retreat upon Christianity, not because it is true or because it is a doctrine of love, but because it would help to keep out the doctrines we fear, that would be a blasphemy. It is true that we shall not survive without a restoration of belief, but it is also true that the restoration of belief can only be spontaneous. It must be of the spirit, guided by the working of the spirit. It must be the spirit of love of God, not that of fear of men, because there is no fear in the Holy Ghost.

This is a moment of history in which it is indeed natural to return to the ground of our being. For an Englishman who loves his country's history, it is natural to count the events of Britain's history as a Christian country, like an old lady counting her rosary beads, from the little wattle church at Glastonbury, which, until it was destroyed by fire in 1184, was the earliest record of Christian worship in Britain, down through the Saints of our conversion such as Patrick and Augustine, through the settlements of the Tudors and Stuarts, to Wesley and Newman. This is the British tradition, a tradition from which a new recurrence of faith can be sought in our time of humiliation.

Yet it is one of the marks of the sterility of the modern world that too many people are cut off not only from their religions but from their past. They do not know where their grandfathers were born or how their grandfathers lived. They have not learned the history of their nation. They may even have a prejudice against history and see the past as old broken-up stuff of no relevance to the modernity of the present.

How can they recapture a tradition of which they are unaware? The history is unknown to them; the doctrines of the religion they have largely lost are unfamiliar to them; the miracles which authenticate that religion are incredible to them; the language of the religion is unfamiliar to their ears; the very idea of religion is associated in their minds with credulity; their lives follow a morality which the religion, if they adhered to it, would require them to change. How can they come back to a religion which has no little apparent hold on their modern lives?

They can only come to it by what they know, and by what is good. They cannot come to it by doctrines they are not ready to understand, or words that have no meaning for them. Yet the central doctrine of the Christian religion, the doctrine of love, everyone knows and everyone understands. It is true that the fear of God is the beginning of wisdom; but it is the love of God which is the beginning of the knowledge of God.

If God wills that the world, after this period of darkness, should come back into the light, it will be the spirit of his love by which the world will be brought back, and it is for this that we ought to pray. This is the spirit of Saint Francis, and it is the spirit of Pope John. It is a spirit accessible to everyone, and everyone is accessible to it.

Everything else in the world, everything else in religion, is secondary to this. The world can only be saved by the love of God which leads to the love of man; without that the world has always been doomed, but we have the assurance and the knowledge that the world will never be without it. That is the assurance of the incarnation of Christ; it is also the assurance of the religious nature of man. We know it from Jesus, and we know it by grace.

Besides this all the cares of the world fade away. If God loves us, and we are even at the beginning of learning to love him, none of the anxieties of this most anxious world can have any hold on us. Those whom God loves need not fear the future, in wealth or poverty, in health or sickness, in freedom or under oppression, in life or in death, for they have something so important that nothing can stand in importance beside it. And God loves everyone.

It is the flooding out of this sense of the love of God which will save the world if the world is to be saved in our generation. And it is by expressing little fragments of this love to each other that we can best help the work.

'The focal point of Rosenzweig's historical thinking is the year 1800 around which cluster the dates of the French Revolution, Hegel and Goethe. The historical perspective offered by these dates suggests to Rosenzweig that the Christian world had entered into its last, Johannine, phase. The notion of Johannine Christianity formed one of the leading ideas of the German idealist movement. It occupied Fichte's mind since 1804, as Hans Ehrenberg has shown. Schelling concludes his lectures on the Philosophy of Revelation with the words, "If I had to build a church in our time, I would dedicate it to Saint John." Peter is the apostle of the Father, Paul of the Son, and John of the Holy Spirit. John represents the church of a free undogmatic Christianity. . . . Its message is one of hope.'
A. Altmann. *Studies in religious philosophy and mysticism.* p. 276 et seq. Routledge and Kegan Paul, 1969.

MR. PAUL JOHNSON, who wrote an excellent biography of Pope John, does not tell us how the name John came to be chosen, and I do not know of any evidence on the question. It was however remarked at the time that John was a name which was somewhat unexpected. There had already been a John XXIII, and he had not been a true Pope. The name was therefore under something of a cloud in the papal succession, as it is in the English monarchy.

It seems unlikely that Pope John was much influenced by the speculations on Johannine Christianity of the German idealist philosophers, and it is much more natural to suppose that he was directly inspired by the example of John the Apostle. Nevertheless it is interesting to note that the impact of Pope John was very similar to the impact of Johannine

Christianity as Schelling and Rosenzweig had foreseen it. They looked at John the Apostle; Pope John looked at John the Apostle; both saw the same thing, and Pope John gave it historic effect.

There are two sources from which Pope John would have formed his picture of John the Apostle. The first of course is the Gospel of St. John. In that Gospel John is portrayed as the disciple whom Jesus loved. He is probably the main source rather than the actual author of the Gospel. He is shown as having a greater intuitive understanding of Jesus than any of the other Apostles; their two minds were open to each other. Jesus on the Cross, in the most moving of all the human incidents of his life, asks John to look after Mary, his mother. It was almost the last thing he did before his death.

'When Jesus therefore saw his mother, and the disciple standing by, whom he loved, he saith unto his mother, Woman behold thy son! Then saith he to the disciple, Behold thy mother! And from that hour the disciple took her into his own home. After this, Jesus knowing that all things were now accomplished, that the scripture might be fulfilled, saith I thirst. Now there was set a vessel full of vinegar; and they filled a sponge with vinegar and put it upon hyssop, and put it to his mouth. When Jesus therefore had received the vinegar, he said, It is finished: and he bowed his head and gave up the ghost.'

(John XIX 26.30)

Jesus gave two trusts to his Apostles: the church he trusted to St. Peter, and his mother he trusted to St. John. To St. Peter we all owe our religion; he is one of the greatest of saints, one of the most loving, and one in whom we ourselves can completely trust. The contrast between him and St. John, or between either of them and St. Paul, is a contrast between different temperaments of men we can wholly admire and love. Yet the differences of temperament are significant.

At the end of St. John's Gospel there is an extraordinary scene. It is after the resurrection, when Jesus has returned to put heart into the disciples. Peter and John and some of the other disciples are at the sea of Galilee and Peter says 'I go a fishing,' so they go a fishing with him. And they do not catch anything all night. In the morning there is a man standing on the shore. None of them recognize him. He tells them to cast the nets on the right side of the ship; they do so and they have a very large catch. John does then recognize him, and tells Peter. Peter is so excited, characteristically, that he jumps into the sea and swims two hundred cubits to the shore (about a hundred yards swim since a cubit is about twenty inches). The others come ashore in a little boat.

When they get ashore Jesus has a meal ready for them. There is a fire and some fish cooking on the fire and some bread. So they bring their catch ashore, which consists of a hundred and fifty three fish, a big catch, and the net is not broken. And Jesus asks them to join him in the meal; they are rather embarrassed because they know perfectly well who he is, but do not like to ask him. He gives them fish to eat and breaks the bread (I suppose from those loaves of flat round bread which are still the bread of Tiberias) and gives that to them also.

Then, after the meal, Jesus asks Peter: 'Simon, son of Jonas, lovest thou me more than these?' and, when Peter affirms that he does, says 'feed my lambs'. And Jesus repeats the question twice more, and Peter is upset to be asked three times, but is given the same charge each time: 'feed my lambs' or 'feed my sheep'.

Jesus then tells Peter of his prospect of martyrdom: 'when thou shalt be old, thou shalt stretch forth thy hands, and another shall gird thee, and carry thee whither thou wouldst not.' It is obvious then that Peter feels at least a trace of quite human jealousy, for he looks at John and says to Jesus 'what shall this man do?' Jesus replies 'if I will that he tarry till I come, what is that to thee? Follow thou me.' This slightly confuses everyone, as it was meant to do. 'Then went this saying abroad among the brethren, that this disciple should not die; yet Jesus said not unto him, he shall not die; but if I will that he tarry till I come, what is that to thee?'

To me, the informality of the conduct of Jesus after the resurrection is one of the most convincing points about it. He is the son of God risen from the dead; if he were a human myth he would surely have behaved with more sense of occasion, and would be resurrected in the grand style, if not in the style of Wagner then at least in that of Handel. Instead two lighter sides of his human character seem to come to the fore, his love of picnics and his ironic sense of humour. He is mistaken for a gardener; he teases Peter, he teases St. Thomas for his doubts, he makes a fire and cooks the fish, he leaves St. John, who has taken his mother into his home, with a riddle, which St. John sees to be a riddle. A God who rises from the dead on the third day in order to cook picnics and make jokes is a God in whose eternal power a poor mortal can be glad to be placed.

Yet there is of course more to it than that. There is a contrast between the role of Peter and the role of John. Peter is to build the church: 'feed my lambs'; it is a task in the world, and because it belongs both to world and spirit, it is a task with powerful temptations which will not always be resisted. Peter had denied Christ three times and his love is questioned three times. In every generation and in every place the church is tempted to deny Christ, not formally but by preferring the appearance of prudence to the reality of love. It is not that Jesus is being unkind to Peter, but that he is putting to the test the rock-like quality of his character, and it is of course upon that rock that all organized Christianity still depends, and the Catholic Church depends in particular. By foretelling his martyrdom Jesus is testing further the character on whose strength everything is going to depend. Peter has the keys of the Kingdom because without him none of us would even know what the Kingdom was, let alone be able to get there.

What did Jesus mean by the riddle about John? John was not quite sure, so we can hardly expect to be sure. Of course John did die, traditionally by martyrdom and in extreme old age. Yet there may be a hint about the historical development of Christianity, that Petrine Christianity is the first phase and Johannine the final phase of the Christian development.

What did John actually preach himself? He provided most of the information for St. John's Gospel, and the transcendant picture of Jesus in that Gospel is how he saw Jesus. How far the distinctive theology of St. John's Gospel is his is a question I am not competent to discuss. We also have the Epistles of St. John. They are very simple and not very long. (The later ones may be wrongly attributed to him.) They sound like Pope John talking. They preach a matured doctrine of Christian love which gives us John's understanding

93

of the meaning of Jesus, that is, the understanding of the man who knew him best.

'Beloved, let us love one another: for love is of God; and everyone that liveth is born of God and knoweth God. He that loveth not knoweth not God; for God is love. In this was manifested the love of God towards us, because that God sent his only begotten son into the world, that we might live through him. Herein is love, not that we loved God, but that he loved us, and sent his son to be the propitiation for our sins. Beloved, if God so loved us, we ought also to love one another. No man hath seen God at any time. If we love one another, God dwelleth in us, and his love is perfected in us. Hereby know we that we dwell in him and he in us, because he hath given us of his Spirit.'

I John 4–7 to 13.

Only a verse or two later the old man repeats:

'Whosoever shall confess that Jesus is the Son of God, God dwelleth in him, and he in God. And we have known and believed the love that God hath to us. God is love; and he that dwelleth in love dwelleth in God, and God in him. Herein is our love made perfect that we may have boldness in the day of judgement: because as he is, so are we in this world. There is no fear in love; but perfect love casteth out fear; because fear hath torment. He that feareth is not made perfect in love. We love him because he first loved us.'

I John 4–15 to 19.

This is the summary of the religious experience of the disciple whom Jesus loved. It is the summary of what Jesus had taught the man who understood Jesus more perfectly than anyone else among the disciples. Christians can live in the light of this doctrine, and are able by this light to understand the whole complex mystery of Christian doctrine.

What we are now again looking for is words which will bring the virtue of Christian truth home to a pagan world; we need therefore the Christian faith not only as organization, or church, the work of Peter, nor only as a complete argument, the work of Paul, but in its distillation. It comes distilled, and at its most personal, in the work of John. This is what Christians say that the world should believe, and that the post-Christian world should again be converted to, the central doctrine that 'God is love, and he that dwelleth in love dwelleth in God, and God in him.' That is not only the central doctrine of Christianity about Jesus; it is the central doctrine of Jesus, as it remained in the memory and was distilled in the meditation of the disciple that Jesus loved.

Again one needs to qualify the argument. If this is taken as an argument against Petrine or Pauline Christianity it fails completely. It would be a hateful falsehood. The Johannine doctrine is implicit in and essential to both Petrine and Pauline Christianity. All the argument amounts to is that Johannine Christianity is the central doctrine of Jesus, stated in its simplest form, and is the particular need of our present age, the aspect of Christianity which has most value as a cure for our failure.

I have no doubt that it was his desire to live out the teaching of John the Apostle in the papacy that made Pope John choose John as his papal name, a choice which has had so much influence that, if one now talks of Johannine Christianity, one is thought to be referring to the Pope and not to the Apostle—a confusion which does not matter as the Pope and the Apostle were of one mind and heart. I have no doubt either that it was the living out of the doctrine of the Apostle that made Pope John the one great international saint of the modern world, the saint known to all nations.

To what degree should Johannine Christianity be regarded as undogmatic, in the sense of the German idealist philosophers? Certainly it has nothing to do with quarrels and disputes over dogma. It is a doctrine of pure love. John did reject certain things without hesitation: 'if a man say, I love God, and hateth his brother, he is a liar;' there is nothing indefinite about that. His belief in Jesus and in the Holy Spirit is profound and self-evident. Yet the emphasis on love as the central experience of religion excludes the possibility of hatred for religion's sake. The whole posture of the inquisitor is condemned by the Johannine standard.

It was therefore natural for Pope John to be ecumenical, just as it was wholly natural for him to be orthodox. He opened his heart in love to all mankind, to Christians of other churches, to Jews, to people of all religions, to people of no

95

religion. Even in Marxism itself he saw the aspects of legitimate idealism, though he did not condone the hatred in it. He feared nothing; least of all did he fear that error should prevail against truth.

There is another reason why Johannine Christianity is relatively undogmatic. It does not alter the doctrines of the Christian religion; it is perfectly orthodox. It does alter their relationship to each other. The pure doctrine of Jesus, as John teaches it, is so compelling, and occupies so large and central a position in our view of Christianity, that other doctrines fall into place around it, true because it is true, and, what is equally important, true in the sense in which it is true.

Take for instance the question of morality, of Christian ethics. This can be seen as a number of separate questions, on all of which there is Christian doctrine. There is a doctrine on social morality, and on the family and on sexual relations and so on. These are important matters and anyone trying to lead a Christian life will care for them, knowing that he will often fall short of Christian standards of conduct.

Then take the single sentence: 'God is love; and he that dwelleth in love dwelleth in God, and God in him.' Apply that to all cases of morality, but apply it with intelligence and realism, and it both enlarges and illuminates the moral code. Remember that God's love is not selfish in the way that human love tends to be; then ask what love suggests in this case or that, and the moral answer often stands out quite clearly. The codes are necessary, and are a very important protection against self-deceit, but they are attempts to codify rules for loving conduct, and owe their authority to that.

Or again take difficulties and doubts. I have no difficulties about the Immaculate Conception, or the Virgin Birth, or the Resurrection or the miracles of Jesus. They are all for me matters of unquestioning belief; yet, wonderful as they are, they all seem to me subordinate to the assertion that God is love; I pray that I shall never be tempted to cease to believe in them, but if I had no knowledge of them but knew that God is love, and that Jesus, his son, had taught us so, I would still not hesitate to call myself a Christian.

Johannine Christianity also opens the hearts of Christians. We are all of us in our human nature hard-hearted, some more so even than others, but all only too much so. Jesus opened the heart of John the Apostle of divine love; in our times John the Apostle opened the heart of Pope John who became the Pope of divine love.

That is how Christians should approach the world. We all shrink from it; for all of us, our imperfect love is not strong enough to cast out fear, particularly the last legitimate fear of the evil that is in ourselves and in others. Yet it is true that Christian love cannot be overcome; it makes Christianity invincible.

This doctrine is also free from puritanism, from that rejection of the world which takes pleasure in avoiding pleasure; the love of God may call for any sacrifice, up to and including the sacrifice of life itself. It may certainly call for the sacrifice of any enjoyment. Yet only for God's sake. The natural response to the love of God is to love all the things and creatures God has made, not instead of God but because of God. Just as John's doctrine casts out fear, so it casts out meanness and that false asceticism which is not for worship but to deprive oneself of enjoyment.

John's doctrine certainly represents a fully orthodox view of sexual morality, provided that morality is based on love, and not on fear or hatred. It is natural for a Christian to see the sacrifice of self required by chastity, either in the priesthood or religious life or marriage, as fully justified, but it is justified by being an expression of love, of love through fidelity in marriage, of love through worship in the religious life, of love through service to others in the pastoral life. Yet sexual love is one of the most ardent expressions of love in human nature. A God of love is not a sort of Christian Venus, a God of erotic instinct, but a God of love cannot be hostile to be expression of love in sexual relationship, so long as it is an expression of love and not of power, or hatred or exploitation of another. But to be an expression of love as a rule requires that it operates inside the terms of orthodox Christian morality. Sexual love which is also love for one's sexual partner tends to seek permanence; and tends to impose sexual loyalty.

The doctrine of John is not designed to distinguish error; in it the sun of God's love shines so brightly that even the fiercest error can hardly darken its light. Yet it does show certain errors in a vivid contrast; they are the dark errors of fear and hatred. Any doctrine which deprives Christian life of joy and hope, *anathema sit*, let it be condemned. Any cutting down of maypoles, or destruction of ordinary pleasures, let it be condemned. Any doctrine of hatred between people is a lie. Any doctrine of God's hatred towards people, or any doctrine that God so hates men as to predestine them to eternal damnation, is an abomination. Any holy war to destroy other people in their homes cannot be the will of a God of love.

In general, Johannine Christianity is Christianity with the strongest emphasis on the positive, on affirmation, on saying yes. There are negative elements in Christianity, elements of caution and prudence which have been necessary for its survival, or may have been necessary for its survival. Taking the whole historical experience of Christianity one can argue that the simple doctrine of Johannine Christianity would not have been enough. But at the same time its strength is that it is free from these negative elements. In a time of hatred John gives us the Christianity of love; in fear, hope; in distress, joy; and always he gives us Jesus and the Holy Spirit. From that a Christian can build a Christian understanding of his own, and will want and will use other elements. There is no end to a deeper or to a broader understanding of Christian belief.

Yet now, talking to an agnostic in an agnostic world, I would not take him to St. Peter's and show him the treasures of church history, deeply though St. Peter's tomb and the great church above it move me. Nor would I offer him the most thoughtful and saintly modern apologetics. I would like him to go back to the Epistle of St. John as a way of approach to the Gospels, and as a summary by his most understanding friend of what Jesus meant. 'No man hath seen God at any time. If we love one another, God dwelleth in us and we in him ... God is love; and he that dwelleth in love dwelleth in God, and God in him. There is no fear in love; but perfect love casteth out fear.' That is the truth of the universe; that is the explanation of the mystery of human life; it is the truth of eternity; it is the truth of God; it is the truth of Jesus; it is the truth of John. To believe in that is what is needed to be a Christian, though many who are not Christians believe it; not to believe in it is to be a lost soul, not lost for ever but lost for now. To accept that is the beginning of the process of christianizing one's soul, and it is to begin to feel the sweetness and the power and above all the truth of the teaching of Jesus himself.

51